# FREEDOM OR SECRECY

# FREEDOM
## or
# SECRECY

◆ ———————————— ◆

*by James Russell Wiggins*

*New York* OXFORD UNIVERSITY PRESS *1956*

*To My Wife*

———————

# PREFACE

---

*Knowledge will forever govern ignorance. And a people who mean to be their own governors, must arm themselves with the power knowledge gives. A popular government without popular information or the means of acquiring it, is but a prologue to a farce or a tragedy, or perhaps both.* — JAMES MADISON *

DURING a period of more than three hundred years, starting with the early years of the seventeenth century and extending into the twentieth century, the people steadily expanded the area about which government conceded they had a right to know.

There were some rebuffs and short-run reverses from time to time; but everything that happened in England and in America seemed generally to work together to enlarge the access of all citizens to information about government itself and to establish in law, custom, and tradition the principle that the people have a right to knowledge and the free use thereof.

In the early years of the seventeenth century, Englishmen commenced to dismantle the vast system of suppression and restriction started by Henry VIII in 1529 with the promulga-

---

* Letter to W. T. Barry, 4 August 1822, *The Complete Madison*, Saul Padover (ed.), Harper & Brothers, New York, 1953, p. 337.

tion of the first list of proscribed books. This system was some
eighty years in the making. It included the licensing of printing, the granting of printing monopolies, the use of religious
injunctions, the resort to star chamber proceedings, the employment of general warrants, the secrecy of Parliament, the
enforcement of savage reprisal for seditious libel and contempt.
Parts of the system were exported to the American colonies.
In a two-hundred-year period most of the bad work of the
preceding eighty years was undone. Some vestiges of this
heritage remained at the start of the twentieth century. Generally, however, the people had established, by law and by the
almost universal acknowledgment of public men, the theory
that the people had a right to know about their own government.

In the United States, the struggle against the sixteenth-
century restrictions proceeded along the same lines it followed in England. Licensing of the press was abandoned.
Doors of legislatures and of Congress were opened. Court proceedings were made public. Laws of seditious libel were mod-
erated and the defenses against libel made available. At local,
state, and federal levels it was conceded that the people had a
right to information.

After three centuries of progress, events seem now to be
moving in another direction. There is abroad in this country,
and in the rest of the world, an impulse to secrecy. It is an impulse which will alter and curb our governmental institutions
if it is not itself altered and curbed.

This retrogression has been caused by military crisis, by
changes in the structure of government, by expansion in the
powers of government, by increases in the sheer size of government, and by declining faith in the theories that made it possible to expand popular rights to knowledge from the seventeenth to the twentieth century.

Legislative, executive, and judicial establishments of local,
state, and federal governments challenge the right of citizens
to scrutinize their transactions. Doors are closed. Records are
sealed. Information is denied.

These actions, if long pursued, will change the character of our government. To appraise what this may do to free government, we need to read again John Stuart Mill's paragraph:

'As between one form of popular government and another, the advantage . . . lies with that which most widely diffuses the exercise of public functions; on the one hand by excluding fewest from suffrage; on the other, by opening to all classes of private citizens, so far as is consistent with other equally important objects, the widest participation in the details of judicial and administrative business; as by jury trial, admission to municipal offices, and above all by the utmost possible publicity and liberty of discussion, whereby not merely a few individuals in succession, but the whole public, are made to a certain extent participants in the government and sharers in the instruction and mental exercise derivable from it.'

We began the century with a free government — as free as any ever devised and operated by man. The more that government becomes secret, the less it remains free. To diminish the people's information about government is to diminish the people's participation in government. The consequences of secrecy are not less because the reasons for secrecy are more. The ill effects are the same whether the reasons for secrecy are good or bad. The arguments for more secrecy may be good arguments which, in a world that is menaced by Communist imperialism, we cannot altogether refute. They are, nevertheless, arguments for less freedom.

In choosing between freedom and secrecy we must remember that each has its risks. Our free ways sometimes are dangerous; but our secret ways are dangerous too. One differs from the other, but is not necessarily less risky than the other.

There is danger that we may choose between them under the illusion that secrecy is safe, and only freedom is dangerous. Or we may deceive ourselves into believing that the two are not incompatible, and into thinking that we can have both freedom and secrecy.

We can have a little of each, to be sure. We can give up a little freedom without surrendering all of it. We can have a little secrecy without having a government that is altogether secret. Each added measure of secrecy, however, measurably diminishes our freedom. If we proceed with more and more secrecy we shall one day reach a place where we have made the choice between freedom and secrecy. We shall pass a point beyond which we cannot go without abandoning free institutions and accepting secret institutions. No man can say with assurance where this point is, but we move toward it.

J. R. W.

*Washington, D.C.*
*July 1956*

# Contents

# Freedom or Secrecy

# 1

## The People's Right To Know About Their Legislatures

*Next to the existence of open constituencies, and a fair mode of election, the best security a nation can possess for the fidelity of its representatives is to be found in the system of parliamentary reporting. But this was also wanting [in the reign of George III]. The theory of the statesmen of the first half of the 18th century was that the electors had no right to know the proceedings of their representatives, and it was only after a long and dangerous struggle, which was not terminated until the reign of George III, that the right of printing debates was virtually conceded.* — LECKY\**

THE people's right to know really is a composite of several rights. It has at least five broad, discernible components: (1) the right to get information; (2) the right to print without prior restraint; (3) the right to print without fear of reprisal not under due process; (4) the right of access to facilities and material essential to communication; and (5) the right to dis-

\* William Hartpole Lecky, *A History of England in the Eighteenth Century*, Longmans, Green & Co., London, 1878, vol. I, p. 442.

3

tribute information without interference by government acting under law or by citizens acting in defiance of the law.

Of these rights, the first in the order of its exercise, and perhaps the first in the order of importance, is the right to get information.

One of the longest and most hotly contested struggles in history was waged by Englishmen and Americans to gain access to their legislatures.

The secrecy of the British House of Commons had its beginnings in the wish of the members to protect themselves against the reprisal of the monarch for words uttered on the floor. The English historian Hume [1] relates that the members so feared the crown that 'they durst use no freedom of speech which they thought would give the least offence.' Queen Elizabeth, in 1589, so roundly abused Sir Edward Hoby that he protested to the House and Commons voted that thereafter no one should reveal the secrets of the House.

By 1642, Parliament was habitually ending its enactments with a brief warning that the parliamentary printer only was to have the right of printing. 'None other,' the House declared, was 'to presume to print.'

Long after the House of Commons had ceased to fear the interventions of the Crown it continued to meet in secret. Lord Macaulay, describing this secrecy as it existed in 1690, said:

All the defences behind which the feeble parliaments of the sixteenth century had entrenched themselves against the attack of prerogative were not only still kept up, but were extended and strengthened. . . The rules which had been originally designed to secure faithful representatives against the displeasure of the Sovereign, now operated to secure unfaithful representatives against the displeasure of the people, and proved much more effectual for the latter than they had ever been for the former.[2]

Various statutes were adopted and different punishments inflicted to enforce secrecy. Even members suffered under some of the punishments meted out.

Arthur Hall, a member from Grantham, for publishing a pamphlet in which he criticized another member for proceedings in the House was called before the bar of the House and sentenced to imprisonment for five months and fined five hundred marks and divested of his membership for a session.[3]

The Speaker of the House, at the same session, admonished the members that 'speeches used in this House by the members of the same be not any of them made or used as table-talk, or in any wise delivered in notes of writing to any person or persons whatsoever not being Members of this House.' [4]

The ban on all parliamentary reporting was renewed by a special ordinance in 1648.[5]

The Parliament of 1649, on 20 September, passed an act declaring that nothing was to be published about government but in official gazettes and the government declared its intention to dispense for public consumption only information it considered fit.

A few weeks after the restoration of Charles II, the Commons passed a resolution declaring that 'no person whatsoever do presume at his peril to print any votes of proceedings of this House without the special leave and order of this House.' [6]

The question of officially publishing votes and proceedings was finally raised in the House in 1680 and, after a debate, the disclosure of the votes only was authorized. Nine years later the House decided to cease publication by a vote of 145 to 180. In October 1689, printing of votes was again authorized. The ban on printing the debates remained. In October 1696, Commons resolved that it was a breach of privilege to print 'as well during the recess as the sitting of Parliament.' In 1723 the House resolved that 'no printer or publisher of any printed paper do presume to insert in any such papers any debates or other proceedings of this House or any committee thereof.'

Early in the eighteenth century, Swift and other writers circumvented the parliamentary interdict by reporting the

proceedings of imaginary deliberative bodies, especially between sessions, in such a manner that the identity of the proceedings and speakers was unmistakable. To stop this, the
House in 1738 declared it a 'high indignity to, and a notorious
breach of the privilege of this House for any news writer, in
letters, or other papers . . . to give therein any Account of
the Debates, or other Proceedings, of this House, or any
Committee thereof, as well during the recess as the sitting of
Parliament.' [7]

While this resolution was being debated, only one member
took a modern view. The Tory leader, Sir William Windham,
while he criticized the accuracy of some reporting said he
had seen many speeches that were fairly and accurately taken
and that, in his view, 'no gentleman, where that is the case,
ought to be ashamed that the world should know every word
he speaks in this House.' He thought that 'the public might
have a right to know somewhat more of the proceedings of
the House than what appears from the votes.' He concluded
by saying that if he were sure that members' views would not
be misrepresented he 'would be against coming to any resolution that would deprive [the people] of a knowledge that is
so necessary for their being able to judge of the merits of their
representatives.' [8]

No one else held these views. The resolution was adopted.

Both the House of Commons and the House of Lords, in
the next decades, moved repeatedly against printers and members for printing proceedings until events of 1771 caused
Parliament to relinquish forever its control over publication.
On 8 February of that year the House of Commons reaffirmed
its customary ban on printing. When it tried to enforce it,
against two London printers, it encountered the inspired opposition of John Wilkes, a London alderman. At the prompt-
ing of Wilkes, the printers' own workmen arrested the printers
and brought them before Wilkes sitting as a magistrate. He
promptly released the printers but held their workmen entitled
to a reward offered by the House and at the same time de-

manded their arrest for assault and false imprisonment. For this mischievous defiance of Parliament, Wilkes, another alderman, and the Lord Mayor were haled before the House. When they stubbornly defended their local rights, they were sent to the Tower. There they stayed until the session ended. The House had had enough of the fight, however, and they were released and the prosecution of the printers dropped. Parliamentary proceedings ever since have been reported without penalty.

Commenting on this long struggle, Lord Acton expressed the opinion that 'public opinion could not prevail while the debates were secret' and pointed out that the press was not really free while it was forbidden to publish and to discuss the debates of Parliament.

Few have made a better short statement of the principles involved than the *London Magazine* which in a 1747 issue, long before the House stopped punishing publication, declared:

Every subject not only has the right, but is duty bound, to inquire into the public measures pursued; because by such an enquiry, he may discover that some of the public measures tend toward overturning the liberties of his country; and by making such discovery in time and acting strenuously, according to his station, against them, he may disappoint their effect. This enquiry ought always to be made with deference to our superiors in power but it ought to be made with freedom and even with jealousy.[9]

The same struggle went on in the American colonies and later in the new government of the United States.

Governor Berkeley arrived in Virginia rejoicing that there were not yet any schools or printing presses in the colony. But in 1682 John Buckner, a merchant and a landowner, brought to Jamestown a printer named William Nuthead. A press was set up and the composition of the acts of the assembly commenced. A this point the printer and his patron were called before the Governor's Council and bound over 'to let nothing pass' until 'the signification of his Majesties pleasure shall be known therein.' In 1684 Lord Howard of Effingham arrived with a royal order that no persons 'be permitted to use any press for printing upon any occasion whatsoever.' The mandate was effective for fifty years, or until 1730 when William Parks started another Virginia press at Williamsburg.

In Massachusetts the whole gamut of English precedent was run, from licensing to secrecy. An Order in Council of 13 May 1725 directed that 'the printers of the newspapers in Boston be ordered upon their peril not to insert in their prints anything of the Public Affairs of this province relating to the war without the order of the Government.' [10]

Legislative deliberations were closed habitually. Finally, the proceedings of the Massachusetts General Court were opened to the public on the motion of James Otis, 3 June 1766, so that citizens might hear the debates on the repeal of the Stamp Act and on the compensation to the victims of the Boston riots.

Samuel Adams, in 1767, circumvented efforts at legislative secrecy when, as the Clerk of the House, he furnished newspapers texts of addresses sent to the Royal Governor.

Pennsylvania witnessed the same sort of struggle. In 1683 the council voted against having the laws of the province printed. In 1689, William Bradford was summoned before the Governor and Council for printing William Penn's charter. In 1719, Andrew Bradford was warned not to print anything about the government when an article he published reflected on the state's credit.

The hostility of New York governments was repeatedly demonstrated and finally climaxed by the case of Peter Zenger in 1734. In his *New-York Weekly Journal*, Zenger criticized the official conduct of Governor William Cosby. He was accused of libeling the Governor. Andrew Hamilton, at his trial, argued that the jury might decide both the fact of publication and the issue of whether or not the publication was a libel. Zenger was acquitted.

Gradually, however, the climate in the colonies changed. Slowly, American governments came round to the view formally expressed by the New York Assembly, which in October 1747 passed this declaration:

Resolved that it is the undoubted right of the people of this Colony to know the proceedings of their representatives in General Assembly and that any attempt to prevent their proceedings being printed or published is a violation of the rights and liberties of the People of this Colony.

Americans so generally supported this philosophy that the secrecy surrounding the Constitutional Convention was much criticized. Typical of this complaint was a letter which Thomas Jefferson, then in Paris, wrote to John Adams, on 30 August 1787, in which he said: 'I am sorry they began their deliberations by so abominable a precedent as that of tying up the tongues of their members. Nothing can justify this example but the innocence of their intentions and ignorance of the value of public discussion.'

There was subsequently plenty of occasion to regret the absolute secrecy of the convention when the states came to approve the great document. It required the Federalist Papers and a great many other postconvention efforts at publicity to overcome the doubt and suspicion and ignorance resulting from secret proceedings.

When Congress first met under the Constitution, on 4 March 1789, the House was open but the Senate met behind closed doors. It permitted the public to hear the discussion of the Albert Gallatin election contest, but did not regularly admit the people to either legislative or executive sessions until 20 February 1794.[11]

On 26 September 1789, the House had an interesting debate on a motion to exclude the press from the chamber. It was alleged that there were inaccuracies in the printed reports in the newspapers. These were admitted but member after member rose to defend the presence of the press.[12]

Elbridge Gerry of Massachusetts was 'in favor of disseminating useful information, by a correct and impartial publication of the speeches.'

John Page of Virginia acknowledged errors in the reports but 'would rather submit to all the inconveniences of ridicule than sacrifice what he thought a valuable publication of useful and interesting information.'

Some members thought the motion to disbar the press 'an attack upon the liberty of the press.'

Misgivings about an authorized, as distinguished from an informal, transcript were expressed. James Madison was among those who did not wish an authorized version of the debates but was against throwing impediments 'in the way of such information as the House had hitherto permitted.'

Another member said he was 'friendly to publishing because it conveyed useful information and gave much satisfaction to those citizens who cannot attend in the galleries to hear the sentiments of those who represent them.'

The House tabled the motion and the press remained. Public access remained on a fluctuating and uncertain footing until 1801 when, by a strict party vote, the Jeffersonians formally admitted the press to both Houses of Congress.

State governments, at the same time, conceded the right of the people to observe the sessions of their state legislatures. Two states have constitutional provisions specifically requiring that the legislatures meet in public, thirty-two states have constitutional provisions admitting the public except in certain circumstances, and the rest, although having no constitutional provisions, do admit the public to sessions.[13]

Most city charters require that meetings of councils and similar governing bodies shall be open at all times to the public.

Notwithstanding these solid constitutional, legal, and historic foundations under the right to know, this right is now being eroded.

Americans do not have the access to the deliberative proceedings of all legislative bodies, federal, state, and local, that they should have. There is a tendency to secrecy. The tendency on the part of legislative bodies does not seem to be limited to the United States. When the House of Commons was debating the creation of a Royal Commission on the press, in October 1946, a member from Huddersfield (Mr. Mallileau) rose to describe this present-day inclination in England. He said:

I have noticed a regrettable tendency in this House and else-where to suggest now, in contrast to what was suggested after the previous war, that it is better to conduct negotiations in secrecy. . . Local councils in some areas, for example, are excluding the Press from their proceedings or, if they are not excluding the Press all the time, they are adopting the trick of turning themselves into a committee of the full council so that the Press cannot get in to see what is going on. This is another way in which freedom of expres-sion and of discussion is hindered, and is something which a Royal Commission might look into.[14]

In the United States, impairment of our right of access to legislative bodies has been caused by:

(1) Delegation of legislative power to executive depart-ments and independent agencies.

(2) Emigration of legislative business from legislative cham-bers to legislative committees, at federal and at state levels.

(3) Increase of secret sessions at local levels of government.

Congress could not escape great delegations of power that is essentially legislative, or rule-making, in a modern, industri-alized urban society in which government is compelled to as-sume increasing responsibility for the detailed regulation of economic activity. While many of its powers have passed over to executive departments, bureaus, commissions, and in-dependent agencies, the protections which surrounded the exercise of legislative power in Congress did not emigrate with the authority to make rules and regulations.

As a result, citizens found themselves increasingly governed by rules and regulations having all the force and effect of law and sustained by penalties for violations, in the formation of which they had enjoyed none of the powers that citizens of a democracy once enjoyed. The rules and regulations were adopted behind closed doors. Citizens had no way of discovering that ordinances which would alter the conduct of their business were impending. They had no way of influencing the character of the rules and regulations while they were under debate. Publication of the completed rules was so irregular that they were not even sure of discovering, except by citation for their violation, what the finished rules were.

Congress took note of this problem and on 11 June 1946 remedied some of these evils by passing the Administrative Procedures Act. Under this statute, provision is made, at least, for notices and hearings and for full publication. Agencies exercising any rule making power can further improve the situation if they act in the spirit of our system and give citizens affected advance notice of intended changes, opportunity to express dissent and influence changes while they are under consideration, and fullest notice of changes once made.

Only by access to legislative committees can citizens nowadays really know what is going on in Congress and in their state legislatures. There was a time when the country was smaller and when the volume of legislation was not great, in which ordinary citizens by attending the sessions of legislative bodies could get a good notion of the legislative process. This no longer is so. What occurs on the floor often is no more than the formal and final confirmation of decisions really made in the closed sessions of committees.

This emigration of effective legislative power, from the floors of legislative assemblies to committees, began to be noticed with disquiet by students of American government shortly after the turn of the century.

Woodrow Wilson became an eloquent critic of secret committee processes. He said:

Legislation, as we nowadays conduct it, is not conducted in the open. It is not threshed out in open debate upon the floors of our assemblies. It is, on the contrary, framed, digested, and concluded in committee rooms. It is in the committee rooms that legislation desired by the interests is framed and brought forth. There is not enough debate on it in the open house in most cases to disclose the real meaning of the proposals made. Clauses lie quietly unexplained and unchallenged in our statutes which contain the whole gist and purpose of the act; qualifying phrases which escape the public attention, casual definitions which do not attract attention, classifications so technical as not to be generally understood, and which everyone most intimately concerned is careful not to explain or expound, contain the whole purpose of the law. Only after it has been enacted and has come to adjudication in the courts is its scheme as a whole divulged. The beneficiaries are then safe behind their bulwarks.[15]

Wilson voiced the bafflement and frustration of many leaders of movements seeking legislative change when he said:

They promise you a particular piece of legislation. As soon as the legislature meets, a bill embodying that legislation is introduced. It is referred to a committee. You never hear of it again. What happened? Nobody knows what happened. I am not intimating that corruption creeps in; I do not know what creeps in. The point is that we not only do not know, but it is intimated, if we get inquisitive, that it is none of our business. My reply is that it is our business, and it is the business of every man in the state; we have a right to know all the particulars of that bill's history.[16]

Practical lawmakers in Congress began to worry about the matter, too. Harold L. Ickes, Secretary of the Interior in the Roosevelt administration, recorded in his diary the very strong opinions of Vice President John Nance Garner on the subject of secret committee sessions. Ickes said: 'Vice President Garner remarked that there ought not to be any executive sessions of any congressional committee. He made the point that it was all public business and that reporters should be permitted to attend any committee meeting.' [17]

This was so much the prevailing view of Congress that when the LaFollette-Monroney Congressional Re-organization Act was passed it provided: 'All hearings conducted by standing committees or their subcommittees shall be open to the public, except executive sessions for marking up bills or for voting or where the committee by a majority vote orders an executive session.' This is Section 133 (f) of the law (Legislative Re-organization Act of 1946).

The committee's understanding of this section, and the public's understanding of it, is plainly stated in the committee report, which says: 'All hearings are required to be open to the public except where executive sessions for marking up bills, or for voting or where the committee by a majority vote orders a secret executive session in the interest of national security.'

This legislation, at the time, seemed a final triumph of the antisecrecy philosophy of Wilson and Garner and other practical reformers of our legislative apparatus. It has been no such triumph.

The 83rd Congress (1953–54) closed 38 per cent of all committee meetings. Press and public were excluded from 1,243 committee meetings out of a total of 3,002 committee sessions. Moreover, the tendency to secrecy seems to be increasing, inasmuch as only 34 per cent of the committee sessions held in 1953 were closed, while 41 per cent of those held in 1954 were closed.

The *Congressional Quarterly* made a complete list of these committee sessions for the periods 3 January to 3 August 1953 and 6 January to 20 August 1954, excluding meetings held during recess, meetings held outside Washington, meetings of conference committees, meetings of the House Rules Committee called to grant rules for consideration of bills, meetings of the House Appropriations Committee and subcommittees of which no record is kept.[18]

Of 1,413 Senate committee meetings, 546, or 39 per cent, were secret and 867 were open. Of 121 joint committee meetings, 70, or 58 per cent, were closed and 51 were open. Of 1,468 House committee meetings, 627, or 43 per cent, were closed and 841 were open.

It is notable that the Armed Services Committee of the House, which might be expected to invoke most frequently the right to impose secrecy for military reasons, held 38 per cent of its meetings behind closed doors, or less than the percentage of secret meetings held by many other committees.

Of the meetings of the Agriculture Committee, 38 per cent were secret, Banking and Currency 42 per cent, Commerce 31 per cent, Education and Labor 92 per cent, Government Operations 54 per cent, Judiciary 62 per cent, Post Office and Civil Service 43 per cent, Ways and Means 70 per cent, Veterans Affairs 45 per cent.

The Senate Armed Services Committee held 55 per cent of its meetings behind closed doors. For some other Senate committees, the score was: Agriculture 46 per cent, Banking and Currency 27 per cent, Commerce 23 per cent, Finance 58 per cent, Foreign Relations 77 per cent, Government Operations 45 per cent, Post Office and Civil Service 47 per cent, Public Works 48 per cent.

The Foreign Relations Committee of the Senate held 75 per cent of its meetings behind closed doors in the 82nd Congress (251 meetings with 63 open and 188 closed). The American Society of Newspaper Editors Committee on Freedom of Information, in May 1953, appealed to the Committee to open more of its sessions. Senator Alexander Wiley, chairman of the committee, promised that the committee would hold public hearings on future legislation and wherever practicable and feasible would open up other hearings to the public. He said sessions seeking background information would remain closed out of considerations of national security. Under this policy, the percentage of closed meetings has increased.

The Finance Committee, which has held 58 per cent of its meetings behind closed doors, was appealed to by the American Society of Newspaper Editors to better inform citizens of its proceedings early in the 83rd Congress. This committee, although meeting in secret, in the past has habitually briefed the press on action taken in sessions on tax bills. There were indications that even this practice would be dropped in the 83rd Congress, but the briefing was later resumed.

Sigma Delta Chi, through its Freedom of Information Committee, headed by V. M. Newton, Jr., editor of the Tampa *Tribune*, has besought all the members of the Senate to open the doors of more committee proceedings. The annual report of the committee included statements from many members of the Senate, sympathetic to the purposes of the committee.

In spite of these efforts, however, it is evident that secret sessions of committees are on the increase, as a part of an apparently almost irresistible impulse toward secrecy in the transaction of public business.

In the states, where the practice of committees varies state by state and committee by committee, the trend is also toward secrecy.

In 1925 North Carolina adopted one of the most advanced access statutes in the country. It provided that the Appropriations Committee of the House of Representatives and the Appropriations Committee of the Senate, and the subcommittees of these committees, were to sit jointly in open sessions while considering the state budget. But in 1953, when citizens attempted to gain access to sessions of these bodies, they were barred. The newspapers of the state pressed their right to be present and the Legislature promptly adopted an amendment to the 1925 statute under which the committees, following public hearings, may hold closed sessions for discussion and consideration of the budget. Final action must still be taken in public. This move back toward secrecy is symptomatic of a tendency in our legislatures.

In the 1953 session of the Virginia Legislature, a resolution under which committee sessions would have been opened to the public failed of passage, upon rejection by the Senate Rules Committee. Subsequently, the lieutenant governor announced that the votes of the Rules Committee, hitherto kept secret, would be recorded and made available.

Hearings are often opened by many legislative committees but the deliberation on measures and the actual voting about which citizens have a vital interest generally are closed in most states.

Local governing bodies, operating under varied local and state laws, still are not generally as accessible to the people as they ought to be in a democracy. Some of these meetings remain closed because the laws are silent on the matter; others operating under satisfactory laws circumvent them by executive sessions or committee meetings.

Authorities on municipal administration seem to be generally agreed that local lawmaking bodies ought to meet in public. The *National Municipal Review* has stated this position well:

> This is a sound, healthy command in a self-governing system like ours. But far too often it is deliberately and designedly modified by city councils and school boards. Legislative bodies have a strong tendency to treat it as just another one of those lovely democratic ideals to which we give lip service but which for 'practical' reasons we choose to ignore. . . It is from debate, discussion and the clash of opinion that the voters learn about their problems and develop an ability to vote intelligently, not from formal ayes and nays.[19]

The Model Charter of the National Municipal League provides that: 'All meetings of the council shall be open to the public.'

Typical of the open-meeting ordinances of the country is that of the city of St. Paul, Minnesota which states:

> All meetings of the council, of all boards, committees and officers, whatever, elected, appointed or employed, shall be public meetings, open to the public under proper regulations to be fixed by ordinances of the council.

Carl H. Chatters, executive director of the American Municipal Association, has plainly stated the view of this group:

> City Councils throughout the United States hold all their official meetings in public. This, I believe, is the universal rule. In thirty years' experience with city government, I have never known of a single city which holds its city council or city commission meetings secretly or in sessions closed to the public.

> No one would dare to contend that a state legislature could appropriately meet except in an open public session. There seems to me to be no more possible justification for city councils or commissions to meet secretly or privately.

Now, it is true that legislative bodies, federal, state and local, must work through standing committees which meet without public notice and sometimes behind closed doors. These same legislative bodies may meet from time to time as a committee of the whole in closed sessions. Even under such circumstances, the official votes and official acts take place at public open meetings.

Closed sessions of a city council would seem to be justifiable only on the grounds that the people of a city had no right to know what the governing body was doing, that the governing body did not wish to be influenced by public opinion.

Nothwithstanding the statutes, the opinions of experts, the demands of the communities to know what is going on, public business all across the country still is being conducted, in all too many cases, behind closed doors.

In cases where the laws are as explicit as it is possible to make them, the formal meetings of governing bodies are reduced to mere pro-forma, confirming proceedings which follow closed and informal sessions in which differences have been aired and debates conducted.

The Milwaukee City Council, in 1954, over the strenuous objections of many citizens, voted to continue closed 'caucuses' preliminary to public proceedings. In 1956 it finally voted to abandon the practice of closed caucuses prior to council meetings.

In other cases, as the result of little-noticed changes in the statutes, meetings hitherto open are being legally closed. In January of 1954, the people of North Carolina discovered that their state legislature in 1951 had quietly amended a law requiring the public meetings of boards of county commissioners. Such frustration of existing law, such circumvention of good access statutes, and such amendment of the laws regarding open meetings, suggest that the basic difficulty is not only in the laws and the interpretations of the law but in public understanding of the reasons for the open conduct of legislative business.

Officials who really do not believe in the public's right to know, despite the statutes to the contrary, probably can perfect the means of conducting the public's business in secret. If there existed a universal understanding of the reasons for open meetings of all sorts of legislative bodies, honest law-makers would not attempt nor honest citizens tolerate devices that effectively deny the right to know about the lawmaking business of the community.

The theoretical considerations and the practical issues in-volved in open legislative meetings need to be restated upon frequent occasion. It must be more widely understood that they are central, not only to the honest conduct of public enterprise, but to the preservation of a democratic system. It is worthwhile to re-examine these considerations in detail. They are restated here not necessarily in the order of their importance, but arranged merely for convenient study.

Legislative bodies in a democracy should meet in the open because:

(1) Public business and not private business is the object of the deliberations of Congress, state legislatures, and local governing boards and commissions of every kind. Citizens have an inherent right to know more about the reasons for restraints and taxes than they can discover from the mere an-nouncement of what someone else has decided.

(2) Legislative power, in a democracy, remains with the whole people, and is only yielded up in part, and for stated in-tervals, to individual citizens acting for the whole people. The whole body of the citizens retains the right to terminate or to renew this grant of power, at certain stated times. This is an empty right at best, and a dangerous one at worst, if it must be exercised by voters who cannot discover how wisely or how foolishly their representatives have conducted the public busi-ness. They cannot discover this without access to the meetings where public decisions are made.

(3) Open proceedings enlist the intelligence of the whole community in the lawmaking process. If a member of a legis-lative body, considering a bill or an ordinance, makes an error in the statement of a premise, in an open meeting, the

community to which the proceedings are reported surely will have some citizen with the specialized knowledge to perceive the mistake, and who will come forth to correct. If the meeting be secret, errors of premise and conclusion may be gathered into a measure without discovery, and on final disclosure it may be too late or too difficult to make needed corrections.

(4) Public proceedings broaden participation in government by citizens as a whole and, in the language of John Stuart Mill, make citizens to a certain extent 'participants in the government, and sharers in the instruction and mental exercise derivable from it.' In addition to drawing upon the wisdom of the community, open proceedings prepare the mind of the community to accept necessary, and perhaps difficult and unpalatable, measures essential to the public good. The civic consciousness of the people is quickened. The appreciation of the difficulties that confront government is sharpened. Their readiness to comply with or submit to necessary measures is increased.

(5) Public proceedings protect the community, the state, or the nation against the possibility of wrongdoing, either by individual lawmakers who may mislead or deceive a majority or by a whole legislative body.

(6) At the same time, they protect the honest and conscientious legislator from successful imputation of wrong conduct by false accusers.

(7) Public proceedings protect a legislative body against being made the victims of fraud or misrepresentation by witnesses appearing at legislative hearings. In a public proceeding it is almost impossible for a witness deliberately to misstate facts without speedy contradiction. The knowledge that this contradiction may be forthcoming serves to check those who might hazard a false tale and assures the correction of those who nonetheless attempt it. The quality of evidence submitted to the lawmakers benefits by both processes.

These advantages of the public conduct of business are not new or novel, but they need to be restated from time to time lest the general principles that make publicity wise are counter-balanced by 'specific expedient' arguments for secrecy.

One of the most popular arguments against open meetings of lawmakers is the contention that business is more efficiently and expeditiously conducted in private. It is often asserted that lawmakers will play to the galleries, resort to tricks of the demagogue, 'ham it up,' protract the discussion, and otherwise obstruct the legislative process.

Legislators who make this argument, by doing so, exhibit a certain sympathetic consideration for the human weaknesses and shortcomings of their colleagues. No one has ever been heard to say that if a meeting is public *he* cannot be depended upon to act like a statesman. None of them ever admits that *he* will play to the galleries or act the demagogue. It is always an anxiety for the conduct of his colleagues. It is a very touching argument for secrecy. It also is a very old one.

Senator William Maclay of Pennsylvania was in the Senate when it voted against opening its doors on 25 February 1791. In his diary he made this entry of his views in favor of open meetings:

The objections against it, viz., that the members would make speeches for the gallery and for the public papers, would be the fault of the members. If they waged war in words and oral combats; if they pitted themselves like cocks, or played the gladiator, for the amusement of the idle and curious, the fault was theirs; that, let who would fill the chairs of the Senate, I hoped discretion would mark their deportment; that they would rise to impart knowledge and listen to obtain information; that, while this line of conduct marked their debates, it was totally immaterial whether thousands attended, or there was not a single spectator.[20]

There are no disadvantages of this kind, in open meetings, that members of legislative bodies cannot correct themselves.

Secrecy sometimes is defended as a means of protecting the good names of individuals against false allegations of wrongdoing that may be made, either by members of a legislative body, or by a witness before such a body. It is an argument that often is invoked by members who exhibit indifference to such considerations by availing themselves of their immunity to attack the good names of citizens with whom they disagree. It is a reason for secrecy that has many sincere advocates.

To its sincere advocates, the best answer is that a man's reputation never is so much endangered as when his conduct is attacked in secret proceedings, by witnesses freed of the restraint of public contradiction, dealing in charges of which he can learn only by rumor.

The most imposing argument against secrecy in a legislative body is that there is no such thing. Members do not have a choice between the fullest secrecy and the fullest publicity. They have a choice between complete, accurate, and honest reports of a proceeding and distorted, inaccurate, hearsay reports of a proceeding. The committees can close the doors, but they seldom can close, utterly, the mouths of their members. They have a choice between an open meeting, fully and accurately reported to all the people; or a closed meeting, reported with varying degrees of accuracy to different groups of the people. So far as such reports are incorrect, they mislead and confuse citizens as to the merits of legislation and the virtues of lawmakers. So far as they are accurate for some citizens and inaccurate for others, these reports constitute a kind of discrimination, and a sort of favoritism that ought to be odious in a democracy.

Secrecy in the consideration of tax measures, for example, is not only open to all the criticism that applies to secrecy in other legislative bodies. There are certain special reasons here why the attempt at secrecy is dangerous to the public interest. When secrecy is attempted, enormous advantage is derived by those who by the excellence of their connections are able to gain intelligence of impending changes before the general public can learn of them. There is a wicked traffic in this kind of information where lawmakers meet in secret. Those who close public meetings, by the very act, confer a franchise and an advantage and privilege upon the few who can gain access and impose a disadvantage upon the many who are not so fortunate.

The people who are governed by the laws need to say to those who make them, in local councils, boards, and commissions, in state legislatures and in Congress, what Woodrow Wilson said about legislative secrecy in 1913:

Those are private processes. Those are processes which stand between the people and the things that are promised them, and I say that until you drive all of those things into the open, you are not connected with your government; you are not represented; you are not participants in your government. Such a scheme of government by private understanding deprives you of representation, deprives the people of representative institutions. It has got to be put into the heads of legislators that public business is public business.[21]

# 2

---

## The Right To Know About Judicial Proceedings

*Everything secret degenerates, even the administration of justice; nothing is safe that does not show it can bear discussion and publicity.* — LORD ACTON *

SECRET arrest, secret trial, and secret punishment are the three prerogatives of arbitrary government that most menace the rights of individual citizens.

Where they are exercised, the individual is helpless. He is unable to assert his rights in any practical way, no matter how much they are promised him in theory.

The protection of public process in judicial proceedings, although it is provided for in the Constitution and asserted in the laws, is under serious threat.

Judicial power has emigrated from the courts, where its exercise is safeguarded by rules, traditions, and fixed procedures, to quasi-judicial agencies in the executive branches of government.

Judicial power has also emigrated to legislative agencies not suited to the trial of issues and not equipped by experience for it.

*\* Lord Acton and His Circle*, Abbot Gasquet (ed.), Burns and Oates, London, 1906, p. 166.

Courts are exercising and are being given increasing powers to close proceedings that judges think will adversely affect public morals.

Types of courts, such as the juvenile courts, are being closed to the public by legislation.

Criminal process, from arrest to conviction, would be far more secretly conducted under rules proposed by bar associations.

Cameras, capable of bringing proceedings to citizens not present in the court room, are being barred under the provisions of Canon 35 and Rule 53.

These departures from open proceedings would no doubt astonish our English forebears who on 19 June 1215 wrung from a reluctant King John, as an article of Magna Carta, the promise that 'the King's courts of justice shall be stationary, and shall no longer follow his person; They shall be open to everyone; and justice shall no longer be sold, refused or delayed by them.' [1]

John Lilburne, who forced open the doors of the court where he was on trial for treason in 1649, merely by asserting that 'all courts of justice ought to be free and open,' would be astonished to discover that his assertion would not move some present-day courts.

Present practices might surprise the authors of the Bill of Rights. No doubt they thought secret trials in America at an end after the adoption of the Sixth Amendment, which states: 'In all criminal prosecutions, the accused shall enjoy the right to a speedy and public trial . . .'

Nothing better demonstrates the firmness with which the generation that framed the Constitution believed in open courts than an attack upon closed courts made in 1822 by Supreme Court Justice William Johnson. Participants in the Vesey slave insurrection in South Carolina, in the panic and hysteria that it precipitated, were tried in closed proceedings. And although Justice Johnson was a large slave owner, and one who defended the institution of slavery, he protested the secrecy of the trials. In a letter to Thomas Jefferson, he wrote: 'I have lived to see what I really never believed it possible I should see, — courts held with closed doors, and men dying by scores who had never seen the faces nor heard the voices of their accusers.' [2]

We have permitted the courts to be closed to us partly because we have forgotten many of the reasons for open tribunals of justice and partly because we have come to esteem more some other advantages to be gained only by secrecy.

The right to a public trial is first of all a right of the accused, but it is not a right of the accused alone, as many lawyers and judges frequently assert. The public trial protects the accused against the undue severity of a capricious court; but it also protects the community against the undue lenity of a capricious court.

At the risk of repeating much that is elementary, perhaps we need to enumerate some of the solid advantages of the open court:

(1) The testimony is improved because the witness is more inclined to tell the truth.

Professor John Henry Wigmore sees open proceedings as improving the testimony subjectively by 'producing in the witness's mind a disinclination to falsify' in the presence of spectators who may be ready to 'scorn a demonstrated liar' or expose a falsehood by later testimony.[3]

Blackstone states the advantage in this manner:

This open examination of witnesses viva voce, in the presence of all mankind, is much more conducive to the clearing up of truth, than the private and secret examination taken down in writing before an officer or his clerk in the ecclesiastical courts, and all others that have borrowed their practice from the civil law; where a witness may frequently depose that, in private, which he will be ashamed to testify in a public and solemn tribunal.[4]

Bentham was equally enthusiastic on the effects of publicity on a witness. He said:

Environed as he sees himself, by a thousand eyes, contradiction, should he hazard a false tale, will seem ready to rise up in opposition to it from a thousand mouths. Many a known face, and every unknown countenance, presents to him a possible source of detection, from whence the truth he is struggling to suppress may, through some unsuspecting channel, burst forth to his confusion.[5]

(2) Testimony is not only improved subjectively by a public trial but it is likely to be increased and enlarged by disclosing new witnesses and calling forth evidence offered in response to or in contradiction of earlier evidence.

(3) The judge, jury, and counsel are, as Wigmore puts it, 'more strongly moved to a strict conscientiousness in the performance of duty' by a public proceeding. He declares his belief that 'in all experience, secret tribunals have exhibited abuses which have been wanting in courts whose procedures were public.'

In the picturesque language of Bentham, publicity 'keeps the judge while trying under trial.' He asserts:

Upon his moral faculties it acts as a check, restraining him from active partiality and improbity in every shape; upon his intellectual faculties, it acts as a spur, urging him to that habit of unremitting exertion, without which his attention can never be kept up to the pitch of his duty . . . under the auspices of publicity, the original cause in the court of law, and the appeal to the court of public opinion are going on at the same time. So many bystanders as an unrighteous judge (or rather a judge who would otherwise have been unrighteous) beholds attending in his court, so many witnesses he sees of his unrighteousness; so many ready executioners . . . so many industrious proclaimers, of his sentence.[6]

No one has more strongly warned against the effects of secrecy on a judge than Bentham when he said:

. . . suppose the proceedings to be completely secret, and the court, on the occasion, to consist of no more than a single judge . . . that judge will be at once indolent and arbitrary; how corrupt soever his inclination may be, it will find no check, at any rate no tolerably efficient check, to oppose it. Without publicity, all other checks are insufficient: in comparison of publicity, all other checks are of small account.[7]

(4) Judges, and other officers of a court, are, by publicity and open proceedings, protected against the imputation of wrongdoing, where they are guiltless of wrong. Bentham warns that when this safeguard is withheld, the reputation of the judge 'remains a perpetual prey to calumny, without the possibility of defense.' With this defense, in his opinion, 'it will in scarce any instance be attempted . . . it will not in any instance be attempted with success.'

(5) Open trials educate citizens as to their rights under the law and as to the means by which they may avail themselves of their rights. Wigmore emphasizes this. And so does Bentham who states:

. . . by publicity, the temple of justice adds to its other functions that of a school . . . a school of the highest order, where the most important branches of morality are enforced by the most impressive means . . . a theatre, in which the sports of the imagination give place to the more interesting exhibitions of real life.

The people thus learn, without being aware of it, he points out, 'the love of justice and some knowledge of the state of the laws on which their fate depends.'

(6) Publicity acquaints citizens, while a trial is in process, of any manner in which the trial may directly affect their interest, and permits them to avail themselves of legal means for their defense.

(7) Publicity for court proceedings operates as a check and deterrent upon others who might be inclined to commit like offenses against the law. They see in the proceedings what the law means to forbid. They are furnished with an example of the consequences of wrongdoing, an illustration of the certainty of punishment.

Notwithstanding these benefits of open courts, many of them repeated again and again by all of the great law-writers, emphasized in court opinions, and entrenched in our laws and traditions, an impulse toward secrecy in all the processes of justice has made great headway in this generation.

It is worthwhile to examine these invasions in the several areas set out at the opening of this chapter.

The delegation of judicial power to administrative agencies is perhaps inescapable in the sort of urban, industrial society in which we live and its inevitability (and constitutionality) has been acknowledged repeatedly in our courts. Yet it carries with it many dangers. James Madison has very appropriately warned that the combination of executive, legislative, and judicial power is 'the very definition of tyranny' and the tyranny is never more dangerous than when it is exercised in secrecy.

The Administrative Procedures Act, referred to previously, has reduced these risks, but even under this protecting law, it is possible for administrative agencies to impose penalties, as a court would impose them, and to do it in a secret manner that would not be countenanced in a court.

Administrative agencies do not always maintain the nice distinction between administrative duties of enforcement and judicial duties of punishment. Enforcement officers are allowed to bring charges, to fix penalties, to stop proceedings where settlement is offered, and otherwise to confuse police and court functions. It is unlikely that very many of such cases come to public notice. Some of them do, from time to time.

Illustrative of such policies is a case that came to light in 1951 and 1952. The Office of Price Stabilization in Washington, D.C., on 12 December 1951, through its District of Columbia office, announced that it had 'found nine Washington grocery and meat stores guilty of ceiling price violations' and that the stores involved had made payments to the government of amounts ranging from $25 to $136 apiece. It stated that names were not being released because the violations were not willful or the result of negligence.

On investigation, it was ascertained that this action was taken in conformity with the OPS *Manual on Enforcement Information*, paragraph 5.3, section A-2:

If a settlement is made for an amount not greater than the over-charge or overcharges (or the best possible estimate of the over-charges), this fact, for the purposes of public information, shall be taken as evidence that the violator has proved to the satisfaction of the Office of Enforcement that the violation was not willful, the result of negligence, or the result of failure to take practicable pre-cautions against the occurrence of the violation, and the *name of the violator shall not be made public.* However, the number of such cases and the cumulative amounts of such settlements shall be re-leased periodically along with an explanation that they have shown beyond a reasonable doubt that no willfulness was involved. While the violator should not be permitted to keep money he has re-ceived in excess of price ceilings, it is believed that publicity in such instances would be unfair to him.

This regulation, on the face of it, seemed reasonable and fair, but it really involved dangerous departures from the rule of open judicial procedures. It was not acknowledged of course, that this was a court proceeding. Lawyers certainly would not think so. To the ordinary layman, however, a govern-ment tribunal at which the citizen can be accused of wrong-doing and in which he can be required to pay the government a sum of money takes on the attributes of a court. The prac-tical objections to the secret levying of fines and penalties are very great. It hardly needs to be pointed out that:

(1) By offering the accused citizen immunity from pub-licity for an alleged wrong (if he will pay an exaction), the government agency, in effect, subjected him to extortion or blackmail.

(2) The business places involved were induced, by the promise of secrecy, to submit to penalties they might have thought unfair and unjust, for alleged violations of which they might not have been guilty.

(3) The patrons of these places of business (if the business places were guilty) were deprived of a knowledge of their irregular practices to which they, as citizens, were entitled.

(4) If the violations resulted from unreasonable regulations, the public was prevented (by secret enforcement) from learning of the faults in the regulations which, as a result,

would continue in effect against other business places. If these regulations were so impractical as to add to the cost of doing business (and to the prices charged to consumers), citizens would never learn of it.

(5) It is not safe to give enforcement officers, or police, the power to make charges, fix penalties, and compose settlements in secret. To do so is to invite discrimination, bribery, and corruption in enforcement agencies.

(6) By announcing that unnamed businessmen in a community had violated regulations, the agency reflected unfairly upon other businesses in the community not at all connected with the offense. Those operating in conformity with regulations are entitled to exemption from blanket accusation of violations, and they can enjoy that exemption only if violators are named.

To all practical purposes, this executive agency put itself in the role of a court, hearing charges, imposing penalties, and compromising cases. Court or no court, a government that can, in secrecy, divest a citizen of any part of his property, is dangerous to individual liberty.

Before its work was completed, OPS thought so, too, for on 13 April 1952 it revised its policy and abandoned its rule of secrecy in such cases.

The *Knickerbocker News* of Albany, New York, in 1952, learned that certain bars in that city had been diluting whiskey. Proceedings were started by the Alcohol Tax Unit of the Bureau of Internal Revenue. The newspaper attempted to get the names of the bars. It was told that the cases had been compromised and the Internal Revenue Bureau declined to give out the names. Charles Oliphant, then counsel for the agency, said, 'the transaction is primarily of interest to the individual and the bureau.' Since then this policy of secret adjustment has been abandoned. It had all the evils of the OPS policy.

Whenever administrative agencies exercise judicial functions, their operations in this area ought to be attended by the same protections of publicity that surround the same processes when they take place in courts.

## Certain Judicial Proceedings

State legislatures seem increasingly disposed to bar the public from certain types of proceedings, making exceptions to the general rules requiring open trials. As Harold Cross has pointed out,[8] 'each exception cuts down, chip by chip, the people's right to witness trials and proceedings in the courts.'

These statutory exceptions include laws closing the courts in cases involving divorce, sex, perversion, and other matters which lawmakers think might either corrupt the public or expose litigants to publicity.

Cross cites the New York statute as typical of one group of states. It provides:

> The sittings of every court within this state shall be public, and every citizen may freely attend the same, except that in all proceedings and trials in cases for divorce, seduction, abortion, rape, assault with intent to commit rape, sodomy, bastardy or filiation, the court may, in its discretion, exclude therefrom all persons who are not directly interested therein, excepting jurors, witnesses and officers of the court.

Real or imagined abuses of the sensational press may have inspired some of these state bans on various types of proceedings. The variety of these laws (and the extent to which they conflict) indicate, as might be expected, that the lawmakers differ greatly on what types of proceedings are 'fit' for the public ear. There is little evidence that indicates the corruption of public morals or debasement of public taste by public trials. There is no evidence of which I am aware to show that citizens of states having such protection against prurience have attained a higher standard of morality than those of states in which the doors of courts stay open for all sorts of proceedings. What goes on in courtrooms, after all, is such a tiny portion of the available sources of the sort of filth legislators find offensive that this ban seems a very ineffectual limitation on the flood of offensive material that is put into print. Even if there is a measurable risk of offending good taste by open court proceedings, it is a risk that has to be weighed against the risk of secret trial. The public dangers of one, surely, on full examination, will appear much less than the public dangers of the other. Secrecy in cases of the sort that legislatures have most frequently found offensive not only puts at hazard the rights of accused persons to a fair trial. It also divests the public of other benefits of public proceedings.

Secrecy in divorce actions, granted in many states, surely encourages this sort of litigation and, in addition, inclines complainants to testimony that they would not dare to make in public in the face of possible contradiction.

Secrecy in cases dealing with sex offenses, for whatever good purposes imposed, tends to conceal from the public knowledge of a widespread social problem with which the statutes generally now deal in a most inadequate way. Fuller public knowledge of these cases, where it has been made available through public attendance at proceedings and public reporting of proceedings, has hastened state policies for dealing with these offenders which are more enlightened and more in conformity with medical knowledge.

Many legislatures have sought to protect the identity of victims of rape attacks. Much can be said for the motives behind such protection. It can be argued that the humiliation of publicity may deter the bringing of complaints. Wisconsin passed such a statute in 1949 and newspapers violating it have been prosecuted for using the names of the victims of rape attacks.* Sound as the motive of the lawmakers may be, how-

* *Editor and Publisher*, 31 December 1949, p. 22. This 1925 law (Sec. 348, 412) prohibited printing names of rape victims. It was first invoked in 1947 against the *Madison Capitol Times* and its editor, William Evjue, for printing the name of a woman who was raped by two men who also murdered her brother-in-law. Judge Roy Proctor of the Dane County Superior Court held the law

ever, even this sort of secrecy has its price, in terms of the public good and the processes of justice.

Some prosecutors fear that such laws may protect complaining witnesses too much. Under such secrecy, irresponsible persons, or accusing witnesses with an axe to grind, may expose innocent persons to all the disadvantages of defending themselves without putting the complainant to much trouble or inconvenience. The crime of rape is a capital crime in some jurisdictions. Perhaps those who allege it has been committed ought to be under all the normal restraints that operate on citizens who bring serious charges. There is a risk that victims will be deterred by publicity from making a charge that ought to be made; but there is also a risk that the utter absence of any publicity will encourage an alleged victim to bring charges that ought not be brought.

Laws that specifically direct secrecy certainly are open to the criticism urged by Harold Cross:

It may well be said that it 'is a humiliating feature of our justice that the Legislature should deem it appropriate to meddle thus in court procedure and that the Courts should endure such meddling.' And 'why not give trial courts an opportunity to exercise their powers and be man-sized judges, instead of constantly twitching wires upon them as if they were marionettes?'

Judges and lawmakers, together, have brought about the closing of a great many courts. National figures are not available. Walter Lister, managing editor of the *Philadelphia Evening Bulletin*, compiled a record of open and closed sessions of all courts in Philadelphia in 1952 and found that of 90,865 sessions of all courts, 53,431 were open and 37,434 were closed. Closed sessions included: Common Pleas divorces 4,103; Juvenile 17,003; Domestic Relations 11,609; Men's Misdemeanance 639; Women's Misdemeanance 1,630; Fornication and Bastardy 1,885; and Adoption 565.[9] It is not likely that Philadelphia is

---

unconstitutional. The State Supreme Court upheld it. Evjue was retried and acquitted. The Legislature has since amended the law to include a ban on broadcasting names of rape victims.

abnormal. Proceedings of this sort are closed in many jurisdictions.

The right to a public trial is a right of the accused but it is not the right of the accused *only*. It also is a right of the public: 'After all, although there is a plaintiff and a defendant in each lawsuit, there is a third entity interested in the outcome of the litigation. We mean the public interest that justice be done.' [10]

The rights of the accused to a public trial have been asserted and reasserted in our courts. The New York Court of Appeals, on 1 January 1954, voted four to two for a new trial of the vice charges brought against Minot F. Jelke because the public was excluded from the trial. In the majority opinion, Associate Justice Stanley H. Fuld said:

Due regard for defendant's right to a public trial demanded at the very least—certainly lacking valid legislative sanction—that he be not deprived of the possible benefits of attendance by the press. Its widespread reporting of what goes on in the courts may well prove a potent force in restraining possible abuse of judicial power.

A typical federal court opinion on the point is that of the Third Circuit, handed down on 3 February 1949:

After mature consideration, we have reached the conclusion, in accord with the present views of the two United States Circuit Courts of Appeal which have passed on the precise question, that the Sixth Amendment precludes the general indiscriminate exclusion of the public from the trial of a criminal case in a federal court *over the objection* of the defendant and limits the trial judge to the exclusion of those persons or classes of persons only whose particular exclusion is justified by lack of space or for reasons particularly applicable to them. Moreover, whatever may have been the view in an earlier and more formally modest age, we think that the franker and more realistic attitude of the present day towards matters of sex precludes a determination that all members of the public, the mature and experienced as well as the immature and impressionable, may reasonably be excluded from the trial of a sexual offence upon the grounds of public morals.[11]

If there are good reasons why the courts should not be closed *over the objection* of the accused, there are also good reasons why they should not be closed at the instance of or with the consent of the accused. The interests of the accused may be adversely affected by closed proceedings, even in accordance with his wishes. Defendants may not be informed about the advantages of publicity or about the dangers of secrecy. A case in the District of Columbia Municipal Court, in April 1950, demonstrated this point. Robert S. Williams, Jr., was accused of indecent exposure, on testimony of two eyewitnesses. He sought a secret trial from which all would be excluded except persons involved in the case. Ruling on the petition for a closed trial, the Court held:

. . . where there has been a waiver by the defendant of the right to require an open hearing, those parties, and only those parties, falling in four general categories have a right to remain in the court room during the progress of the trial. The first category is the parties to the action and their counsel. The second category is the officers of the law. The third category embraces members of the bar; and the fourth category embraces representatives of the press.[12]

By allowing the press to remain, the judge permitted newspaper accounts of the trial to reach the public. These reports, which indicated clearly as the trial progressed that the accused was about to be convicted, so disturbed the man really guilty of the offense that he came forward and acknowledged his guilt and agreed to submit to psychiatric treatment. Williams was freed, as the result of the publicity he had strenuously sought to prevent.

It may be fairly asked if an accused person ever ought to be allowed to prejudice his own interest by a closed trial even if he wishes to do so.

And apart from the interests of the accused are the interests of the community at large in the fair administration of justice. The secret procedures of a court actually may serve the interests of the accused; but they are nonetheless offensive. The United States Court of Appeals for the District of Columbia vacated a sentence because the lower court had permitted a plea in mitigation to be made in chambers instead of in open court. In doing so it cited an English case where a witness had been interrogated by the court in the absence of the defendant, and quoted the Lord Chief Justice as saying:

That is a matter which cannot possibly be justified. I am not suggesting for one moment that the Justices had any sinister or improper motive in acting as they did. It may be that they sent for this officer in the *interests of the accused;* it may be that the information which the officer gave was in the interests of the accused. That does not matter. Time and again this court has said that justice must not only be done but must manifestly be seen to be done.[13]

The New York courts, in 1954, in the so-called Jelke cases, held the public without a right to access to judicial proceedings as long as the defendant's right to a public trial was upheld. Newspapers of New York tried to assert the public right to an open trial, but the Court of Appeals of the state held that the closed Jelke trial 'did not deprive petitioners of any right or privilege.'[14] The court said: 'The public's interest is adequately safeguarded as long as the accused himself is given the opportunity to assert on his own behalf, in an available judicial forum, his right to a trial that is fair and public.'[15]

In a dissenting opinion, Judge Charles W. Froessel said: 'The right of the public to attend a criminal trial, like the right of an accused defendant to a public trial, stems from the deep roots of the common law.'[16]

The New York courts, later in 1954, held that they could not require the clerk of the Kings County court (New York Post *v.* Samuel S. Liebowitz) to furnish the *New York Post* with a transcript of the charge which Judge Liebowitz delivered to the jury in a criminal case. Production of the transcript, they held, could be compelled only in behalf of prosecution or defense, but not in behalf of newspapers or ordinary citizens. These New York opinions strike a blow at the theory that access to judicial proceedings is a right of the public as well as a right of the accused.

In the latter case, however, the Appellate Division of the

Supreme Court, while averring that it lacked power to compel
the lower court to provide the public with a transcript, did
assert a public interest in such records to this extent:

To permit widespread reporting by the press of what goes on in
the courts, whether by access to the actual trial or to the transcripts
of all or any part of the stenographic minutes of the proceedings
is of substantial value. By providing a contemporaneous review in
the form of public opinion, it may prove a potent force in the effective restraint of possible abuse of the judicial power. It permits
the public to judge whether our system of criminal justice is fair
and right. It prevents the judiciary from a suppressing, editing or
censuring of events which transpire in proceedings before the courts.
It permits the public to know how their servants conduct the public's
business.[17]

Ohio courts, meanwhile, were taking a position in behalf of
the public's right to know about judicial proceedings.

The Ohio Court of Appeals on 12 April took the view that
the right of access to the courts is a public right as well as the
right of a defendant. The newspapers of Cleveland sought a
writ of prohibition against Common Pleas Judge Parker
Fulton, who allowed a defendant to waive his right to a public
trial and at the defendant's request cleared the courtroom of
spectators.[18] In granting the writ, Appellate Judges Lee E.
Skeel, Joy Seth Hurd, and Julius Kovachy said:

A defendant has no right, constitutionally or otherwise, to a private
trial—that is, one hidden from the public view.

. . . Courts are public institutions. They are maintained by the public as a necessary part of the process of government in maintaining
order and adjudging the legal obligations and rights of the people.

. . . Any suggestion that law enforcement has any private aspects
as to the manner in which justice is administered is completely without foundation. To permit trials of persons charged with felony to
be held in secret, the order of secrecy being based entirely on defendant's request, would take from the court its most potent force
in support of the impartial administration of justice according to
law.[19]

The Ohio Supreme Court subsequently declined to set aside the Appellate Court writ.

## Cooley on Public Trials

One of the authorities most frequently cited by lawyers and judges to sustain the view that the rights of defendants and not the rights of the public are concerned in open court proceedings is Judge Thomas M. Cooley.

Often quoted is a statement from his *Treatise on Constitutional Limitations,* declaring:

The requirement of a public trial is for the benefit of the accused; that the public may see he is fairly dealt with, and not unjustly condemned, and that the presence of interested spectators may keep his triers keenly alive to a sense of their responsibility and to the importance of their functions; and the requirement is fairly observed if, without partiality or favoritism, a reasonable proportion of the public is suffered to attend, notwithstanding that those persons whose presence could be of no service to the accused and who would be drawn hither by prurient curiosity are excluded altogether.[20]

This paragraph often is cited as though the opening sentence read 'for the benefit of the accused ONLY.' Of course, it does not say that at all and it does not seem possible that this is what Judge Cooley meant. The quotation is taken from a section of his great treatise dealing with 'protections to personal liberty,' and, in this context, it is naturally the rights of the accused that would be emphasized primarily. In opening this very discussion, however, Judge Cooley says: 'It is also requisite that the trial be public.'

Elsewhere in this work, in discussing privilege, he states:

The law, however, favors publicity in legal proceedings, so far as that object can be attained without injustice to the persons immediately concerned. The public are permitted to attend nearly all judicial inquiries, and there appears no sufficient reason why they should not also be allowed to see in print the reports of trials, if they can thus have them presented, as fully as they are exhibited in court, or at least all the material portions of the proceedings impartially stated, so that one shall not, by means of them, derive erroneous impressions which he would not have been likely to receive from hearing the trial itself.[21]

At another point he states:

Trials at law, fairly reported, although they may occasionally prove injurious to individuals, have been held to be privileged. Let them continue to be privileged. The benefit they produce is great and permanent and the evil that arises from them is rare and incidental.[22]

Elsewhere Cooley says, 'the public demand and expect accounts of every important meeting, of every important trial, and of all events which have a bearing upon trade and business, or upon political affairs.'

The theory that Cooley held a public trial to be the right of the accused only is not consistent with the language he did use in referring to the rights of defendants nor is it consistent with the remarks made at other points in his treatise.

Among cases he cites to illustrate his point, moreover, is People *v.* Hartman, in which the court states:

The trial should be public in the ordinary common sense acceptance of the term. The doors of the court room are expected to be kept open, the public are entitled to be admitted, and the trial is to be public in all respects, as we have before suggested, with due regard to the size of the courtroom, the convenience of the Court, the right to exclude objectionable characters and youth of tender years, and to do other things which may facilitate the proper conduct of the trial.[23]

It seems unlikely that Judge Cooley would have adverted to this opinion, with its emphasis on the fact that 'the public are entitled to be admitted,' if he had held the view that this was a right of the accused only.

The defendant who is willing and able to press his right to a public trial, under numerous opinions of the state and federal courts, stands upon very solid ground.

The public, the ordinary rank-and-file citizens, asserts that right in the courts with increasing success, notwithstanding reverses such as those suffered in the New York state courts.

All of the benefits and protections deriving from the public conduct of the courts will not be safe in the people's possession until the statutes, in those jurisdictions where court opinions have been adverse, are modified to make it plain that the right of access to judicial proceedings is a right which the legislators have intended to confer upon citizens who have committed no crime as well as upon those who have been charged with an offense.

## The Juvenile Courts

Courts dealing with juveniles seldom admit the public. Nearly all state legislation dealing with the subject provides for secrecy of proceedings and records.[24]

Typical of the statutes governing proceedings involving minors is that of the District of Columbia. The Juvenile Court Act, as amended by the 82nd Congress, states in section two:

> In the hearing of any case, the general public shall be excluded and only such persons as have a direct interest in the case and their representatives shall be admitted except the judge, by rule of court or special order, may admit such other persons as he deems to have a legitimate interest in the case or the work of the court.

The philosophy behind this secrecy, which has been on the increase since the turn of the century, has been frequently stated. It is alleged that the tribunals dealing with minors are not really courts, but social agencies dealing with the cure and rehabilitation of the young. It is contended that publicity would interfere with rehabilitation and reform.

At hearings before the Senate Subcommittee on Juvenile Delinquency, Judge Edith Cockrill of the Juvenile Court of the District of Columbia well expressed this philosophy:

> Under the law the child coming before the court is given certain protections such as privacy of court hearings and the protection of his court records and contracts. This is to insure the opportunity for rehabilitation without fear of public criticism or the stigma of a court record. And I want to emphasize at this point the juvenile court's legal and moral responsibility for providing this protection

and likewise to say that I think the letter and spirit of the juvenile court law requires that equal protection be afforded by the police and such other institutions and agencies as may deal with these children. A moral responsibility in this respect also rests upon the public press.[25]

The basic arguments for secrecy have been summarized by Fred W. Woodson, Director of the Juvenile Court of Tulsa County, Tulsa, Oklahoma, who has stated:

1. The whole structure of juvenile court philosophy is based on the premise that children should not be treated as mature adults. For this reason, we have separate statutes, separate tribunals, separate detention facilities.
2. Publicity may result in the child's being ostracized by his peers and even by his family; ostracism is not a corrective measure. Publicity creates shame and embarrassment, often subjecting innocent members of the family to mental torment . . .
3. Publicity frequently magnifies the seriousness of the offense, thereby creating additional problems for the child to overcome . . .
4. Publicity can work in reverse. While it ostracizes one youngster, it glorifies another, who may try to live up to the infamy he has gained and prove he deserves his reputation as a 'big shot'; and it may encourage his peers to admire and emulate him. A child may intentionally commit a delinquent act in order to see his name in print . . .
5. Publicity leads to the way to prejudgment . . .[26]

In the past few years, however, many have begun to express doubt as to the wisdom of the degree of secrecy that has come to prevail generally in juvenile court proceedings.

In 1946, Governor Mortimer B. Proctor, of Vermont, vetoed a bill that would have prohibited publication of juvenile delinquency commitments, in a message asserting:

A prohibition against publicizing juvenile cases could result in improper or illegal commitments being innocently or secretly made. Such a prohibition, instead of protecting and shielding the juvenile, might operate to his disadvantage. . . Publicity is a deterrent to crime and in some cases brings retribution to the parents who so often are primarily responsible for such delinquency. The public should know how our juvenile courts, our probation and enforcement officers, are functioning, and it is only by the spoken, written or printed word that such knowledge may be brought to the public attention. Frank discussion should be encouraged and not throttled.

The Juvenile Court Advisory Committee of the District of Columbia, on Thursday, 8 July 1954, held a special committee meeting to reconsider the policy of secrecy under which its court operated. On Friday, 7 January 1955, the Juvenile Court admitted newspaper reporters to proceedings under an agreement binding them not to use the names of juveniles or otherwise violate the spirit of the Juvenile Court Act.

The Virginia General Assembly, at its 1952 session, modified its juvenile court statute to except from secrecy proceedings involving adults and to permit the judge to admit persons having an interest in a trial.

The 82nd Congress (1952) amended the District of Columbia law to give the judge some discretion in deciding what proceedings and records might be opened and to whom they might be opened.

Professor John Henry Wigmore has stated both the reasons for secrecy and the cautionary note that should have kept us from carrying secrecy too far:

The modern juvenile court rightly relies upon kindly paternal spirit in its procedure, as a necessary means to reach the emotions of the delinquent and to secure candid avowals and ready amenability to treatment. With this purpose, it seeks to eliminate the usual incidents of a criminal court, particularly the strict formality and tense combativeness. Privacy of examination of the delinquent and his family is therefore regarded as generally useful and occasionally essential; and statutes usually provide for this.

But in so far as such statutes make privacy compulsory, or so far as practice habitually exercises the power, it has its dangers. No court of justice can afford habitually to conduct its proceedings strictly in private. The reasons above given are as applicable to juvenile courts as to others. The tendency to undue privacy should be checked.[27]

If we are to check 'the tendency to undue privacy' we must re-examine the philosophy that has led to its imposition and see if the experience of the last generation, under a policy of relative secrecy, has had all the good results anticipated for it, and see if it has had any bad results.

Juvenile crime has been on the increase throughout the whole period of this experiment. The increase has been sensational in the last few years. Yet it would be unsafe and unwise to assume that secrecy was wholly to blame or that the increase might not have been greater if older methods had been used. Perhaps the most we can conclude is that secrecy, in any case, has not diminished the amount of juvenile crime. To give it any measureable blame for the increase would be to minimize all the social, economic, and political factors that have made for more juvenile crime and for the more efficient reporting of such offenses.

The dangers of secrecy ought to be kept in mind, however, in weighing present practices and legislation.

First, there is the obvious and apparent danger that attends secrecy in any court. All of the considerations that argue for publicity in courts generally apply with equal effect to this court. The rights of the accused are better protected (and the accused in this instance is a litigant who does not know of his rights or how to avail himself of them). The quality of the evidence is improved. The good conduct of the court is made more likely. The public is kept informed of the manner in which the court operates.

Secondly, secrecy has removed the deterrent effect of publicity. Whatever its psychological disadvantages, publicity has some constructive effect upon citizens. Its greatest effect is precisely upon the class of offenders here involved, its least effect upon hardened, professional offenders. Its importance is greatest in large urban areas where the individual otherwise enjoys a degree of anonymity that he would not have, in any case, in a small or a rural society. The normal person covets the good opinion of some group of relatives or friends. The certain assurance that these persons will have instant knowledge of wrongdoing is a restraint upon the impulse to disregard the laws, customs and conventions and mores of society. The assurance that wrongdoing by a juvenile will not be made known to the community must measurably diminish this deterrent. Police officials are well aware that gangs of youthful offenders frequently count upon the minor's immunity to publicity. Those under eighteen are chosen for the overt act, the actual breaking and entering, the direct commission of an offense. Sometimes, police believe, they are encouraged to assume blame for offenses of older youth. If secrecy means enough to youthful lawbreakers so that they will contrive to put the blame on those who are immune to publicity, it seems safe to infer that the uniform publication of the names of offenders would have some deterrent effect. In explaining the amount of crime among American troops in the European Theater of Operations during World War II, Judge Advocate General E. C. Betts emphasized the effects of a 'loss of identity' upon individual behavior. He pointed out the consequence of removing individual soldiers from communities where their wrongdoing would be known to friends and relatives and concluded: 'If anyone is among friends or people he knows, and wants their respect, he hesitates before doing anything shameful.'

By assuring young people that their wrongdoing will not become known to friends or people they know, we have diminished this natural hesitation. We have conferred upon individual youngsters the dangerous advantages of anonymity.

The social workers, and those they have persuaded to adopt secrecy, believe that publicity interferes with reform, that anonymity furthers rehabilitation. This is a theory that needs some further examination. It has disadvantages even if it is correct. In order that we may deal more effectively with the reform of boys and girls who have violated the law, we have dropped a device that has heretofore operated to keep boys and girls from violating the law. In order to diminish the likelihood that a first offender will commit a second offense, we have multiplied the possibility that the individual will become a first offender. Even if it worked, it would be a doubtful advantage and there is a good reason to doubt that we have cut down even the number of repeaters.

A third, and the most serious, consequence of secrecy is its effect on public information. As Senator Robert C. Hendrickson of the Senate Subcommittee on Juvenile Delinquency puts it, 'We have failed in large part to get even our own elementary understanding of the problem over to the man on the street.' We have swept the problems of youth in crime under the community rug. As a result, public and private agencies having to do with these problems, in almost every community, lack funds, facilities, and personnel. The District of Columbia, for example, has shortages in every field of its work. Social workers attached to the juvenile court have twice the case load they should have. Playgrounds that might keep youngsters out of trouble often are closed for lack of attendants. Probation workers have time enough to visit only a fourth of the homes of their charges. The staff available for psychiatric care of juveniles is only half that required by existing cases, which often wait six months to a year for treatment. The child guidance staff should be twice as large. There are only 133 public health nurses and 275 are needed. The Health Inspector has 29 employees and needs 55 more.[28] These shortages are typical.

Society does not always act to solve the problems of which it knows. It is better informed about adult crime, but there still is far too much of that. However, knowledge is the essential preliminary to action. If it sometimes does not act with knowledge, it surely never acts without it.

The nameless, faceless, anonymous statistics which are furnished citizens do not call forth their understanding. If the people as a whole could see for themselves, or through the eyes of competent and trained observers, what judges and court attendants and probation workers see every day, something would be done about the appalling shortages that have deprived modern methods of dealing with youthful crimes of a fair chance to prove themselves.

A fourth and final aspect of the doctrine of secrecy that needs to be restudied and re-examined is the assumption on which it rests—the assumption that the people, if informed, will not support enlightened methods of dealing with the crimes of minors. The policy commences with the premise that the people, if told about a minor offender, will demand that he be punished instead of reformed, and will exhibit toward the individual child a hostility that will prevent his return to society. Is this pessimistic picture of humanity a fair, accurate, and honest one? Is the people a wretched, mean-spirited, retaliatory beast, filled with angry impulses and purposes of retribution? Or is humanity generally disposed to look with some indulgence upon youthful offenses, to be tolerant about the missteps of youngsters who have been handicapped by environment and training?

The reaction of the American public to all these problems in recent years suggests that they are inclined to be helpful, not obstructive; kind and not cruel; generous and not stingy; enlightened and not benighted; wise and not foolish.

It is very doubtful that a democratic people, by secrecy, can be persuaded to support policies that they do not understand. If they oppose enlightened policies, the proper way to put them into effect is not to pursue them secretly, but to educate the people to believe in them. By trying to skip this process of education, the advocates of the new approach to youth in crime have insulated the people from problems about which they should have firsthand knowledge. Government never will be able to cope with juvenile crime until it is handled in a way that calls forth the interest, compassion, cooperation, and support of all the people.

## Pre-Trial Publicity

The United States Constitution guarantees both a free press and a fair trial. In recent years, many lawyers and judges have expressed fear that one was being sacrificed to the other. To prevent this, they have sought, by various means, to restrict public access to and comment on criminal cases during the interval between arrest and trial and to restrain lawyers from comment on cases in the courts.

A pattern for this sort of restriction in the United States was set by the Criminal Court of Baltimore in 1939. Later, other Baltimore courts gradually adopted the rules then prescribed in the court of Judge Emory H. Niles and formalized them under Rule 904 of the Supreme Bench of Baltimore City. The rules forbid: (1) photographing the accused without his consent; (2) official statements by state authorities or counsel for the defense relative to the conduct of the accused, admissions or statements by the accused, or any other matter bearing on the issues to be tried; (3) statements as to any future course of action by prosecution or defense; and (4) publication of any matter tending in any manner to interfere with the administration of justice.

The Maryland Court of Appeals held the rule invalid (Rule 904) when it was invoked against Baltimore radio stations for their reporting of a murder case. The Maryland high court handed down its decision 10 June 1948. The United States Supreme Court later declined to review the state court decision.

In March 1953 the Maryland State Senate passed a measure introduced by Senator Francis X. Dippel of Baltimore under which state's attorneys and other law enforcement officials would have been restrained from discussing any criminal case with press or radio 'while such case is pending in the trial courts.' The measure was defeated in the House.

The New York State Bar Association on 26 June 1954 adopted a resolution urging amendment of its own and the American Bar Association's Canon 20 which prohibits lawyers in pending criminal cases from giving statements to newspapers which might interfere with a fair trial. A proposal urging legislation to make it unlawful for opposing counsel and officials to make disclosures in any criminal case 'unless authorized by the court' was referred back to committee.

The American Bar Association on 20 August 1954 adopted a resolution requesting its Committee on Professional Ethics and Grievances 'to study and report to the House of Delegates at the earliest practicable date upon a proposed amendment to Canon 20 of the Canons of Professional Ethics, which would condemn as unprofessional press releases and public statements, the publication of which may interfere with a fair trial in the courts or the due administration of justice.'

The existing language of Canon 20 states:

Newspaper publication by a lawyer as to pending or anticipated litigation may interfere with a fair trial in the courts and otherwise prejudice the due administration of justice. Generally they are to be condemned. If the extreme circumstances of a particular case justify a statement to the public, it is unprofessional to make it anonymously. An ex parte reference to the facts should not go beyond quotation from the record and papers on file in the court; but even in extreme cases it is better to avoid any ex parte statement.

Edwin M. Otterbourg, president of the New York County Lawyers Association and chairman of the American Bar Association committee on unauthorized practice of the law, has urged a joint law-press code on fair trial and free press. His code would ban: (1) opinions on pending cases; (2) statements that would impair public morals or corrupt young readers; (3) statements by attorneys on what they propose to prove or statements criticizing court or jury; (4) press statements on what witnesses are going to say; (5) press comment on credibility of witnesses; (6) sensational headlines; (7) matter excluded from the jury; (8) facts concerning the discreditable acts of a person prior to the crime involved; (9) reports of a confession until it is received in evidence; (10) reports on attitudes of particular jurors following a trial; and (11) press efforts to influence a judge during trial.[29]

These proposals, on the whole, are in imitation of the restrictions that British courts have imposed upon the press. There, virtually nothing can be published between the arrest of a suspect and his trial. It is illegal to refer to the prior record of an accused man. There can be no reference to a confession before it is given in evidence.

The press, before accepting English practice as a model, has seen fit to ask first if criminal justice is ideally administered in England and second if the environments are strictly comparable. A. T. Burch, associate editor of the *Chicago Daily News,* has submitted some answers to these two initial questions. On the first point, he has written:

Are the British so law-abiding because their criminal procedure is so effective? Or is their procedure so effective because the people present it with few and simple problems? It does not work with absolute infallibility. Last year, they hanged John Christie for murdering six women over a period of years. He confessed all these crimes and the court believed him. The trouble is that the British had already hanged another man for killing two of these women. England, remember, is a country where an editor can be fined for assigning his own men to investigate a case and publishing the findings after a suspect has been arrested. It is quite possible that, if some enterprising crime reporters had worked on the case, they wouldn't have hanged the wrong man before they hanged the right one. In the United States, certainly, many an innocent man owes his liberty or even his life to the enterprise of investigating newspapermen.[30]

Mr. Burch also emphasizes the great difference between the problem in England and in the United States by quoting Virgil W. Peterson, director of the Chicago Crime Commission, who has stated that there were, in 1952, in the City of London and all its suburbs nineteen armed robberies, while Chicago with less than half the population had 4,400 armed robberies. The English experience seems hardly relevant to American conditions.

Before considering the merits of the bar proposals, it seems logical to ask if there has been widespread and substantial denial of the right to a fair trial. Have the courts, under the impact of the complained-of American practices of press and bar, convicted large numbers of innocent persons of crimes of which they were not guilty?

Many such convictions must have reached the United States

Supreme Court and have been reversed there if this were so, unless the Supreme Court, too, has been corrupted by un-ethical newspapers and lawyers. There has been, in recent years, only one notable such reversal (Shepherd *v.* Florida, 341 U.S. 50). Nor do our courts, on the whole, seem to be convicting courts. Virgil Peterson has pointed out that Chi-cago, in the past twenty-five years, has had 700 gang murders, and the convictions obtained as a result of them can be counted on the fingers of both hands. Even in cases that have provoked the most public comment on pre-trial and trial reporting, such as the Sheppard murder case, the courts have not held that rights of the accused were denied. On the record, and on the evidence cited by lawyers themselves, it is somewhat difficult to understand the pressure for more stringent control of bar and press in the handling of criminal cases.

What is the merit of such proposals as those made by Mr. Otterbourg?

Many of them have much merit. Several of the provisions of his proposed code are adhered to by many newspapers and followed by many lawyers, at their own discretion. Many newspapers habitually avoid statements that might be designed to persuade either judge or jury, shun forecasts of what a witness will say, avoid conclusions as to the credibility of wit-nesses, eschew sensational headlines, suppress courtroom state-ments excluded from the jury, do not allude to a prisoner's prior criminal acts, defer publication of confessions until submitted in evidence, avoid polling juries, and scrupulously refrain from attempting to influence a judge. Many of these provisions of the code are enforceable under contempt, with-out any further rules or restraints.

Other newspapers may violate many of these rules.

Few newspapers would suppress all factual statements that would tend to 'impair public morals or have a corrupting effect upon young readers' because few persons would agree when statements essential to a full report of a trial have such effects, and even if they do (in the view of some persons) it might be impossible to report a trial fairly without using such facts. Nor would many newspapers agree never to poll a jury, after a case, as long as such polls frequently disclose the corruption and bribery of juries.

The merits of these proposals, however, are not the central issue on which press and bar divide. The spokesmen for the Otterbourg rules and for Canon 20 changes believe the restraints they urge can be put upon publication without interfering with the right of citizens to know about their own law enforcement processes. Newspaper spokesmen and critics of the bar do not think so.

Because other professions have adopted enforceable codes of ethics, lawyers think newspapers should do so. No association or compact of newspapers in history ever has agreed to such voluntary rules. It is not likely that any ever will. In Jefferson's language: 'Our liberty depends on the freedom of the press and that cannot be limited without being lost.' It was, of course, Jefferson's view that it cannot be limited by law. It is equally doubtful if it could be limited without being lost if the limits were set by newspapers themselves. Without some sort of sanctions which some official body could impose, any code would be no more comfort to the bar than the Canons of Journalism or the toothless provisions of Canon 20. With any kind of sanctions, individual newspapers might be destroyed for publications made in violation of a code, but in the public interest.

The bar proposals would guarantee those who administer justice that they would be under greatly diminished scrutiny from the time of a prisoner's arrest until his trial. Sometimes, publicity in this interval may prejudice the rights of the accused. Other times, it is only the knowledge that the press is a constant observer that keeps enforcement officials from overzealous efforts to secure evidence or obtain confessions. The fact that the plight of an accused person, in this country, is kept constantly in the public mind, after arrest and before trial, is not wholly to the disadvantage of the accused. It is unlikely that an accused person will be maltreated, abused, or deprived of his rights while the public, in effect, is looking on. Where the people are not allowed to forget a prisoner, authorities are not as likely to forget him—or his rights. So too, where there is public scrutiny, there is less chance that accused persons will obtain by bribe or influence discriminatory treatment, or even unlawful release from detention.

To protect against undue severity or undue laxity, there must be full access to information about the law enforcement process from the commission of a crime until disposition of the completed case.

One of the most important safeguards against the abuse of police power is publicity for arrests. This is the rule in most American jurisdictions, but efforts continue to be made to clothe arrests in secrecy.

The Georgia Legislature, in January 1955, had presented to it a bill under which it would have been made a criminal offense to publish or broadcast the names of persons arrested for a long list of crimes, including rape, sodomy, and other sex offenses, until indictment or arraignment. The measure was inspired by the wish to protect accused persons against publicity and grew out of the reports of the arrest in 1954 of some well-known persons. Its effect, of course, would be to jeopardize the rights of all accused persons. Prisoners taken in secret, closely confined, and denied access to friends or counsel cannot assert their rights. If friends and family do not even know where or why they are held, such constitutional protections as habeas corpus become purely theoretical and unrealizable rights.

In June 1954, the Department of Health, Education and Welfare tried to get Congress to amend a bill requiring that District of Columbia arrest books be kept open, so as to permit secrecy in the case of books maintained for recording the names of juveniles who are arrested. Proponents of the amendment were willing to give access to 'interested' parties, but not to the public.

Notwithstanding the opposition of the Department, the bill was passed without the amendment, and in its final form included a model section under which citizens can enforce their right of access to arrest books by mandatory injunction issued by the United States District Court. Congress refused to close any part of the arrest docket, but the arguments of the Department of Health, Education and Welfare illustrate the kind of pressures against the right to know about law enforcement that frequently have prevailed.

This controversy also demonstrated how little understood are the reasons for the fullest publicity of arrests. We need to re-examine, frequently, the reasons why no free society can tolerate secret arrests. The open arrest book affords the citizen a vital protection against arbitrary government or corrupt government. Here are some of the ways in which it protects the citizen:

(1) It protects the citizen against the likelihood of arrest without cause. The police, knowing that each arrest must be recorded, and may have to be explained, are naturally reluctant to use arrest powers frivolously. Where there is no record of arrest or detention, citizens who are arrested and released have no public record to back up their attempts to gain redress.

(2) It protects the individual citizen against illegal detention. If there is no record to disclose that a citizen has been apprehended, an individual can be picked up and held without access to relatives, friends, or lawyers and deprived in fact of all the rights of due process assured him in theory. The entry in the arrest book, to which the people have full access, is the individual's assurance that his disappearance will not go unnoted, the cause of his detention unmentioned, and the means of his defense unprovided.

(3) It protects the community against the release of arrested persons through pressure and influence. It is a safeguard against improper release of those arrested for good cause. The arrest book entry (alteration of which is a crime in most jurisdictions) makes unavailing the efforts of those with

power, influence, and money to secure release. Because the police, in the face of the record, dare not dismiss prisoners without authority, the integrity of the police also is protected.

(4) The open arrest book protects the integrity of criminal statistics, upon which the public knowledge of the whole problem of enforcement rests. The Federal Bureau of Investigation, for many years, has maintained uniform crime reports which have been invaluable in estimating trends in crime, suggesting revision of the statutes, and determining the efficiency of law enforcement agencies. The only clear check on the accuracy of statistics for any jurisdiction is the arrest book. Access to precinct arrest books in Washington, in 1947, disclosed that the Metropolitan Police Department was withholding reports on crimes of violence and thereby distorting its crime solution record. When name-by-name checks of arrest books divulged that nearly half of some categories of crimes were going unreported, the crime reporting procedures of the department were revised to conform to FBI standards. From these disclosures came public attention to the policies of the Metropolitan Police Department, and in the wake of that public attention came personnel and policy changes that have transformed the department as a law enforcement agency. If any category of lawbreakers is exempted from publicity or omitted from the public arrest books, a name-by-name check of books against statistics becomes impossible.

The most fearful aspect of a police state is the power of authorities to seek out an individual, seize him without cause or explanation or disclosure, hold him without notice to friends or family or counsel, and dispose of him without explanation or apology. The open arrest book is the citizen's best defense against this menace and it never will be abandoned or abridged by a democratic people aware of their own rights and the means of safeguarding them.

If publicity is important at time of arrest, it is also important at subsequent phases of the process of determining the guilt or innocence of an accused person. The bar frequently protests publicity of confessions prior to submission in evidence and with some good occasion complains that this prejudices the mind of the community—and of a jury subsequently to be chosen from the community. Many newspapers take care that they do not describe as a 'confession' declarations and statements by arrested persons. Publicity for such statements occasionally benefits the community and accused persons. Disclosure that authorities claim to have obtained from an accused person certain admissions of guilt frequently has been the means of exposing police resort to duress in obtaining such statements. Sometimes it has divulged inconsistencies in the alleged admission of an accused person that, called to public attention, have uncovered more accurate information on a crime.

Even statements by prosecutor and counsel concerning their intentions, although occasionally prejudicial to a case, have in some instances exposed to the community, in advance of trial, weaknesses in a case or unfitness in a prosecutor.

It is to be hoped that members of the American bar always will worry about circumstances that might tend to prejudice the right of an accused person to a fair trial. It would be most unjust to say of lawyers thus concerned what the old jingle said of the lawyer:

> The lawyer with a client that's raped
> And but for news of it escaped,
> Is never much inclined to think
> So very well of printer's ink.

Lawyers, and newspapers and others as well, are rightly concerned about the aspects of some sensational trials.

The remedy, however, certainly is not less publicity for the law enforcement process. If we could obtain testimony on this head from all the unfortunate prisoners of the catacombs of ancient Rome, the cells of the Tower of London, the corridors of Old Bailey, the chambers of Lubianka, Dachau, and Buchenwald, that testimony surely would be: 'Do not give to your government the power of secret arrest, secret trial, or secret punishment.'

## The Camera in Court

The camera is not permitted to record the proceedings of any federal court or those of state courts in twenty-eight states.

Its use in federal courts is barred by Rule 53 of the Rules of Criminal Procedure adopted by the United States Supreme Court, which states:

The taking of photographs in the courtroom during the progress of judicial proceedings or radio broadcasting of judicial proceedings from the courtroom shall not be permitted by the court.

Its use in the state courts of twenty-eight states is barred by various forms of Canon 35, promulgated by the American Bar Association, which states:

Proceedings in court should be conducted with fitting dignity and decorum. The taking of photographs in the court room, during sessions of the court or recess between sessions, and the broadcasting of court proceedings are calculated to detract from the essential dignity of the proceedings, degrade the court, and create misconceptions with respect thereto in the mind of the public and should not be permitted.

The use of the camera, by press and television, to bring to citizens throughout the land, and the world, eyewitness reports of proceedings otherwise not available to them has become such a commonplace that the same access is now being sought to judicial proceedings.

In recent years, press and television cameras have recorded for countless millions of persons far removed from the events involved incidents ranging from birth to death. The people have seen, through the camera lens, demonstrations of modern surgery, actual scenes of battle, the Eucharistic mass, almost every ritual of every religious faith, legislative bodies in action, the President and other executive officers of government engaged in tasks ranging from cabinet sessions to cornerstone laying. They have seen courts in action, too. They have not been able to witness, by this means, federal courts or state courts in twenty-eight states.

Some lawyers and editors believe the canon should be continued as it is, notwithstanding the increased use of the camera to record other events. This point of view recently was stated in the *Journal of the American Judicature Society* by an eminent judge who said: 'So far as I can see, the canon needs no change. Proper enforcement of the canon will in no way impede the proper discharge by the press of its ancient duty to fully and fairly report the news and will help us all to conduct the proceedings in our courts with fitting dignity and decorum.' [31]

The same position is taken by many newspaper editors, including the author of this paragraph in the *Bulletin of the American Society of Newspaper Editors:* 'Any judge with any wisdom and a backbone will protect the proceedings in his court from the abuse of radio and television showmanship. If there is faltering on the part of the judges, let us hope that the abuse will be forbidden by legislation.' [32]

There are thus differences within both professions most directly involved, as well as between them. There also is a wide area of agreement on what the camera should not be permitted to do in the courtroom.

No one advocates the uncontrolled, indiscriminate use of old-fashioned, flashbulb equipment in the courtroom. It is agreed that this type of equipment, hitherto conventional with press cameramen, disturbs the court, distracts witnesses, interferes with decorum, and otherwise prevents the orderly conduct of judicial proceedings. It also is generally agreed that the work of a trial court cannot proceed in premises cluttered with conventional motion picture and television cameras, requiring extra lighting, noisy recording equipment, and other devices that noticeably intrude on the court.

Those who advocate the use of the camera in the courtroom are arguing for the use of cameras that will not disturb the court, the witnesses, the accused, the jury, or the audience in the courtroom. The judge must be satisfied that the equipment to be used will meet these standards.

Opinion on photography even under these circumstances is still divided. Many judges think that Rule 53 and Canon 35 need to be revised so as to permit modern camera equipment under conditions of which individual courts approve.

That camera equipment might some day meet the standards of the most scrupulous judge seems to have been anticipated by the joint bar-press committee which in 1937 framed the resolutions out of which the American Bar Association's Canon 35 emerged. That joint committee consisted of six members of the bar, seven representatives of the newspaper publishers, and five editors. They were convened shortly after the coverage of the Bruno Hauptmann trial had greatly disturbed American opinion. The committee was unanimous in recommending that '. . . the use of the cameras in the court room should be only with the knowledge and approval of the trial judge.' [33]

The present-day argument really resolves itself into an argument over whether now, with all the improvements that have taken place in camera equipment, judges should be given the discretion that the joint bar and press committee thought they should have (but the American Bar Association didn't think they should have) nearly twenty years ago.

Many distinguished judges believe that trial judges should be given this authority in both federal and state courts.

Judge Johnson J. Hayes of the U.S. District Court for the North Carolina Middle District has made the best statement of the case for the use of the camera in federal courts. In an address at Raleigh, North Carolina, in 1954, he said:

. . . the people are not only entitled to such information as may be supplied by a free press but by any other modern means for the distribution of information. I am unable to see why freedom of the press which, when it was included in the law of the land, was the recognized medium for the dissemination of information, should be restricted to the instrumentality of the print shop; a liberal interpretation would extend the guaranty to the radio, photography and television. These modern means of spreading information have gained wide popularity. Indeed many will listen who will neither read nor look, and vice versa . . . The founders of our government felt that the safest protection for the preservation of liberty was informed citizenship and they were determined to perpetuate the untrammeled right for the citizen to get that information by securing a free press. If their purpose was to preserve the free and untrammeled right of the citizen to be informed, that right inherently extends to such media as radio, photography and television.

The state courts not governed by Canon 35 have been able to experiment with the use of camera equipment in the reporting of trials.

Judge Saul I. Rabb of the Criminal Court of Marion County, Division Two, Indianapolis, Indiana, has permitted photographers in his courtroom under conditions that have furnished a good test of the effects of the camera on a trial.

Photographers were allowed in the 1954 trial of Victor Lively, who was found guilty and sentenced to life in prison. The judge told cameramen they could take all the pictures they wished to but told them to take no flash pictures while the jury was in the courtroom, and not to get near the jury box or between the prosecutor or defense attorney and the witness when testimony was being given. William Herman, a photographer for the *Indianapolis News*, used a Leica camera with a 135 mm lens and new fast film, getting most of his pictures from a distance of thirty feet or more. After the trial, Judge Rabb said there never was a time during the trial when he felt that the photographers were hampering the dignity of the court or interfering with the jury.

Of as great interest was another proceeding in the same court in 1948 when Judge Rabb permitted the use of flash equipment and powerful lights in a burglary trial. At the end of the trial, the Judge set aside a guilty verdict because he felt that the excitement caused by the flash pictures gave the case more prominence in the minds of the jurors than the evidence indicated. That experience prompted him to allow no flash pictures thereafter while the jury was in the room.[34] Judge D. W. Bartlett of the 54th Judicial Circuit permitted newspaper, television, and newsreel cameras to photograph the trial of Harry L. Washburn, on a charge of murder, in proceedings at Waco, 6–9 December 1955.

Following the trial, questionnaires were sent to all lawyers of the Waco–McLennan County Bar Association. This question was asked: 'In your opinion, did the following detract from the dignity of the court, distract the witnesses or jury, or otherwise disrupt the orderly procedure of the trial?' The answers were tabulated as follows:

|                      | Yes | No  | Per Cent Answering Yes |
| -------------------- | --- | --- | ---------------------- |
| Press Photographers  | 10  | 39  | 20.4%                  |
| Still Photographers  | 9   | 37  | 19.5%                  |
| Movie Photographers  | 10  | 35  | 22.2%                  |
| Television           | 5   | 47  | 9.6%                   |
| Spectators in Court  | 7   | 40  | 14.9%                  |

Of 41 lawyers who answered a questionnaire asking which type of coverage was the least disrupting and disturbing, 65.9 per cent favored television, 34.1 per cent press reporters.

Of the lawyers submitting answers, 92.9 per cent favored allowing reporters in future trials, 76.7 per cent would allow still photographers, 68.5 per cent would allow movie cameras, 87.5 per cent would allow television.

Forty-seven out of sixty lawyers who answered thought the admission of cameras ought to be left up to the judge.

Other state courts in Oregon, Iowa, Tennessee, Arizona, and North Carolina have permitted photographers, operating without flash bulbs and with new fast film, to take pictures during the trials, with results satisfactory to the court.[35]

Other state courts have firmly opposed the use of the camera, some even in the vicinity of the courtroom.

The Ohio Supreme Court on 27 January 1954 adopted this rule:

Improper publicizing of court proceedings — Proceedings in court should be conducted with fitting dignity and decorum. The taking of photographs in the court room during such proceedings and the broadcasting or televising of such proceedings tend to detract from the essential dignity of the proceedings, distract the witness in giving his testimony, and create misconceptions with respect thereto in the mind of the public and should not be permitted.

When the *Cleveland Press* took photographs in the court of Common Pleas Judge Joseph H. Silbert in August 1953, the city editor, a photographer, and a reporter were cited for contempt. They were found guilty of contempt and the Ohio Supreme Court refused to grant a rehearing.

The Colorado District Judges Association, in March 1954, adopted a 'Rule 27' under which photographs were not to be permitted in courtrooms even during recess. This was set aside by the Colorado Supreme Court on 3 September 1954.

On 27 February, 1956, the Colorado Supreme Court, following hearings conducted and recommendations made by Justice O. Otto Moore, decided to permit judges to allow the use of cameras in the courtroom under circumstances in which the trial judges think there will not be interference with order and decorum.

In New York state, photographers were refused permission to take pictures in a courtroom while the room was being used by the Moreland Commission, investigating race track scandals. A photographer for *Newsday*, a Long Island daily, was put out of the hearings and had his camera confiscated for taking photographs covertly.

The courts of Westmoreland County, Pennsylvania, on 25 February 1954, adopted a rule prohibiting photographs 'inside the courthouse during any session of the court, or the recesses between sessions' and stating that:

. . . no person, litigant, prosecutor, defendant, plaintiff, claimant or respondent, juror or witness shall be photographed or have his or her or their pictures taken in a court room or in any of the halls, corridors or approaches thereto during any session of the court or recesses between sessions, and no prisoner, or inmate of the county jail shall be photographed in the jail or in any of the approaches thereto or on his way to or from a session of court.

Newspapers sought to enjoin the enforcement of this rule and, failing this, seven newspaper executives, reporters, and photographers, in January 1955, deliberately invited arrest in order to obtain a high court review of the Westmoreland County rule.

There is no longer much dispute about the ability of cameramen to take photographs without interfering with the trial proceedings or upsetting the decorum or order of the court in any way. Roy Matherly, a photographer for the *Greensboro Daily News*, took pictures of the trial of Mrs. Mae Atkins in Guilford Superior Court, on 9 December 1954, and accomplished his task so inconspicuously that long afterward Judge Burgwyn, sitting on the case, summoned a reporter to his bench and asked when the pictures were going to be taken. There have been similar experiences in other courts.

Argument persists as to other effects of the photographic record on the accused, the witnesses, the jury, and the public. Some judges and lawyers fear that the mere knowledge that photographs are being taken will cause witnesses to be confused and distracted.

Judge Saul I. Rabb of the Criminal Court of Marion County, Indianapolis, Indiana, whose experiences with photographed and televised proceedings have been related, thinks this is not so. In a letter written shortly after a trial which was televised and photographed, Judge Rabb said:

It is my opinion that they have no effect on jury or witness. If the photographer or newspaper reporter conducted himself as outlined in the published article (25) the jury will not pay attention to the pictures being taken, and witnesses will not think of the newspapermen or photographers, as there is nothing to direct their attention to them.

I have always felt that the words 'Public Trial' in the Constitution meant much more than personal attendance of the public. To me it means a trial so that the entire public may know what is going on in the Courts, which they, the public, as tax-payers, support and maintain. There is not a regularly constituted courtroom which can hold or seat all the people in its county. I make this statement to impress that 'Public Trial' means, not some of the people, but all of the people are entitled to the 'Public Trial' mentioned in the constitution.

Since this is impossible, then there must be a media through and by which the public can be appraised of the activities of their courts. This media in the past has been newspapers. Courts must keep pace with Science. There are many Supreme Court decisions sustaining the viewpoint that Courts must keep abreast of Science and the Courts should take advantage of the Radio, TV, newspapers and photographers, the use of which gives the public and the litigants a public trial in the broadest meaning of the constitutional provisions of a 'Public Trial.'

Mine is a Criminal Court with a small courtroom, and a maximum of 75 people can attend any trial. This is a community of 500,000. Seventy-five people attending, in a community of 500,000, is not a public trial, in my opinion, within the meaning of the Constitution.

I feel that the entire public is entitled to the news of its Courts which includes pictures of the proceedings.

Persons not accustomed to speaking in public places no doubt are somewhat bothered by a courtroom audience, as they would be affected by the jury or the judge alone. Whether this discomfiture is measurably increased or not is a question that is difficult to answer. One would think that the impersonal lens of the camera would dismay timid persons less than spectators in whose countenances the self-conscious witness must see, or imagine that he sees, signs of disapproval or censure.

Equally in dispute is the question of whether or not the camera, and the larger audience to which it gives access, inspires the 'show-off' on the witness stand to grab for public attention. Here again it seems doubtful that the invisible audience would measurably alter the influence on the witness of the visible audience in the courtroom.

Some lawyers have feared that the camera would increase the inclination of counsel to 'ham it up' in their examination of witnesses or in argument. Few of them fear that they themselves would yield to such a gross impulse. They do not name lawyers they think might be so inclined. Still they fear there might be some lawyers influenced in this manner. It seems doubtful that counsel with such proclivities could resist an audience as big as a jury. There really is no evidence that there is any law of behavior in which 'the bigger the audience the bigger the ham' is the rule.

If the televising of trials becomes routine in American practice, TV will face, in more pressing form, some of the difficulties that already confront the press. It will have to take care that prosecution and defense are presented in equal balance, in order to protect the privilege of telecasts. And discretion surely must be exercised to see that the literal copy of the proceedings does not convey, out of the context of a whole trial, a false impression. These challenges have been handled by the press and no doubt can be handled by TV.

Properly employed, there seems little reason to regard the camera, which makes the public outside the courtroom witness to what goes on in the courtroom, as an innovation any more startling than the hearing aid, which permits the spectator in the rear row to hear testimony that otherwise would be inaudible to him.

Judge Saul I. Rabb has pointed out its virtue as a means of literally enlarging the courtroom and thereby multiplying all the advantages claimed for public proceedings by Wigmore, Bentham, and Blackstone. That virtue becomes a greater one in an age in which fewer and fewer people, in relation to the whole population, have the opportunity to attend the sittings of the courts.

The televised courtroom, in this sense, makes practically possible the real meaning of the words, 'public trial.' The printed and the televised image, obtained without any interference with the court, is available to enlarge 'attendance' at every public trial. It seems unlikely that Canon 35 and Rule 53 will keep out of American courtrooms permanently the spectators they now ban.

## 3

---

## THE RIGHT TO KNOW ABOUT THE
## EXECUTIVE DEPARTMENT

*Wherever any public business is transacted, wherever plans affecting the public are laid, or enterprises touching the public welfare, comfort or convenience go forward, wherever political programs are formulated, or candidates agreed on, — over that place a voice must speak, with the divine prerogative of a people's will, the words: 'Let there be light!'* — WOODROW WILSON *

*The entrance gates to records [in executive departments] are shut and guarded except on those occasions when official grace is moved to set them ajar for light and air.* — HAROLD CROSS †

THE right of citizens to know about the conduct of their own government, to see for themselves the public records of the executive departments, certainly seems implicit in all the

* Woodrow Wilson, *The New Freedom,* Doubleday, Page & Co., New York, 1913, p. 134.

† Harold Cross, *The People's Right To Know,* Columbia University Press, New York, 1953, p. 183.

theories of democracy and self-government upon which our system rests.

Equally implicit in our system, however, as deeply embedded in our traditions and as extensively elaborated in our laws, is the right of the President, in the absence of express provisions to the contrary, to decide what records of the executive departments may be withheld and what disclosed.

For more than 150 years, this restless contradiction has persisted in our theories, our policies, and our statutes.

The federal government was not a year old (13 May 1790) when Senator William Maclay of Pennsylvania asked the United States Treasury Department for the receipts Baron von Steuben had given for funds advanced to him. Alexander Hamilton demurred and Maclay reported in his diary: 'I told him any member of Congress had a right to any papers in any office whatever; that as chairman of the committee I had promised to procure what papers were necessary.' [1]

Maclay told Hamilton that 'the papers I wanted belonged to the public and to no private gentleman whatever, nor would it do for him to refuse information to a committee of Congress.'

Nevertheless, Maclay did not get the papers he sought. Hamilton evaded and dodged, but still refused.

Curiously enough, the principles upon which the refusal was based were first stated with most clarity by Thomas Jefferson, in refusing to yield up the Burr papers to Chief Justice John Marshall:

With respect to papers, there is certainly a public and a private side to our offices. To the former belong grants of land, patents for inventions, certain commissions, proclamations, and other papers patent in their nature. To the other belong mere executive proceedings. All nations have found it necessary, that for the advantageous conduct of their affairs, some of these proceedings, at least, should remain known to their executive functionary only. He, of course, from the nature of the case, must be the sole judge of which of them the public interests will permit publication. Hence, under our Constitution, in requests of papers, from the legislative to the executive branch, an exception is carefully expressed, as to those which he may deem the public welfare may require not to be disclosed; as you will see in the inclosed resolution of the House of Representatives, which produced the message of January 22nd, respecting this case.[2]

The principle was restated, and the philosophy of other Presidents consistent with it summarized, in a memorandum which Attorney General Herbert Brownell submitted to President Dwight D. Eisenhower, on 17 May 1954. In the course of this memorandum, Brownell said:

For over 150 years, almost from the time that the American form of government was created by the adoption of the Constitution, our Presidents have established, by precedent, that they and members of their Cabinets, and other heads of executive departments have an undoubted privilege and discretion to keep confidential, in the public interest, papers and information which require secrecy.

Brownell stated in the memorandum noted above: 'The courts too have held that the question whether the production of the papers was contrary to the public interest, was a matter for the Executive to determine.' The House Committee on Government Operations, on 27 April 1956, challenged some of the Brownell statements in a staff study entitled *The Right of Congress To Obtain Information from the Executive and from Other Agencies of the Federal Government.*

Executive refusals to give Congress information were described as a 'mere naked claim of privilege' on which, the committee print said, 'the judiciary has never specifically ruled.' The same study also emphasized that courts have not distinguished basically between executive agencies and quasi-legislative or quasi-judicial agencies. It claimed judicial precedents show that the President has been held to be subject to the power of subpoena of the courts (although the only recourse against him is impeachment). The committee experts also argued that 'any possible presidential immunity from the enforcement of the legal process does not extend to the heads of departments and other federal agencies' and claimed that the courts have 'never recognized any inherent right in the heads of Federal agencies to withhold information from the courts.'

Congress, whatever the merits of the constitutional dispute, has allowed discretion in the executive department, both by desisting from efforts to get executive papers, and by enactments such as 5 U.S. Code Annotated 22 authorizing the executive agencies to exercise custody over their files and papers. The present legal situation is thus fairly summarized:

In the present state of the law the people and their organs of information must trust primarily to official grace as affected by reason, courtesy, the impact of public opinion, and other non-legal considerations and, in the longer view, to remedial legislation by Congress. As of now, in the matter of *right* to inspect such records, the public and the press have but changed their kings.[3]

The situation is somewhat redeemed by decisions of the state courts asserting the right to determine what state executives may or may not withhold.* It has been improved in the federal establishment by the Administrative Procedures Act (5 U.S.C.A. 1001–11) concerning the administrative agencies set up by Congress. It is being somewhat altered by some express provisions in statutes requiring publication. The legal situation, however, generally is as dark as Harold Cross paints it, and for a full presentation of the existing legal predicament, readers should consult his book *The People's Right To Know*.

In interpreting the principle enunciated by Jefferson and repeated by so many of his successors, two important considerations need to be kept in mind.

* The Arizona Supreme Court in 1953 required the Governor to disclose certain information regarding an investigation of the State Land Commissioner in an opinion stating: 'Certainly this court will not go so far as to approve the position of the Attorney General that the Governor of the state is the sole judge as to what information regarding the affairs of his office should be made public. This, we believe, is inconsistent with all principles of democratic government . . . It rests within the jurisdiction of the courts of the state to determine these questions. . .'

The presumption that the people do have a right to know about the executive establishment was so strong at the time of the adoption of the Constitution that both Congress and the courts called upon executive agencies for records in their care very early in the history of the government. The executive, in responding to these requests, felt required to state an exception — the records and papers which in the executive's opinion 'he may deem the public welfare may require not to be disclosed.' The presumption of public right, in principle, remains. It persists in the face of the assertion that it is the executive who must determine when the right is to be allowed and when it is to be denied. This is a far cry from universal secrecy, and a long remove from countenancing unvarying secrecy. The language of Jefferson, and that of many of his successors who have withheld information, dealt with exceptions to what they acknowledged by implication to be a general rule.

This general rule, to be sure, is not stated anywhere in the Constitution. The presumption in its favor, as a principle, was so strong 150 years ago that Jefferson felt called upon to explain exceptions, and the people still are entitled to an explanation of those exceptions which the executive can justify in the public interest.

In the constitutions of some free countries this right is expressly affirmed in the constitution. The Swedish constitution specifically provides:

To further free interchange of opinion and general enlightenment, every Swedish citizen shall have free access to official documents in the manner specified below. This right shall be subject only to such restrictions as are demanded out of consideration for the security of the realm and its relations with foreign powers, or in connection with official activities for inspection, control or other supervision, or for the prevention and prosecution of crime, or to protect the legitimate economic interest of the State, communities and individuals, or out of consideration for the maintenance of privacy, security of the person, decency and morality.

The specific cases in which official documents are to be kept secret, according to the aforementioned principles, shall be closely defined in special legislation enacted jointly to the King and the Riksdag.[4]

When the general principle is thus stated, of course, there must also be a statement of precise exceptions to it (as there is in the Swedish constitution) and these exceptions become, in fact, an authorization to withhold information in certain areas.

In effect, it has been our method to begin with a broad presumption of right, permit the executive to decide the exceptions to that right generally, legislatively state some areas in which the executive may not disclose and legislatively prescribe some situations in which it must disclose. The information sub-committee of the House Committee on Government Operations has been considering several proposals to make more effective the legal right of citizens to get information from federal executive agencies. Some of these measures contemplate a new assertion of the public's legal right to know, a general description of areas in which the executive right to withhold is acknowledged, and devices for determining in the courts whether a given executive refusal to disclose is or is not justified.

By whatever method a given people proceed, it is clear that the effectiveness with which citizens enjoy the right to know about their government, in the end, will depend not only upon the laws but upon the genius of the people, the climate of the times, and the extent to which those who govern acknowledge that they are indeed the servants and not the masters of the governed.

The citizens have the means of encouraging this philosophy. The fact that they do have it, in the power of the ballot, probably explains why the presumption in favor of the right to know still persists, despite the weakness of the law.

Throughout our own history, alongside the legal elaboration of the right of executive exceptions to disclosure has run a practical assertion of the right of people to know. Jefferson, whose views on withholding certain papers have been stated, was equally firm in asserting the government's duty to inform. In urging the publication of some executive charts and papers in 1800, he wrote:

I cannot suppose the administration can have any objection to the publication of the charts, etc. My own opinion is that government should by all means in their power deal out the material of information to the public in order that it may be reflected back on themselves in the various forms into which public ingenuity may throw it.[5]

The want of the strict legal power to enforce disclosure, in the face of executive refusal, has been offset not only by the general acknowledgment of this 'duty' in democratic government; it has been balanced, as well, by the practical necessities of governing. Successive executives have prudently refrained from pushing the power to withhold information to a point where the want of the means of compelling disclosure would produce demands for legal remedies. The power to withhold has been neatly set off by the wisdom of disclosing.

The enormous growth of the executive establishment has multiplied rather than diminished the necessity for disclosure and the wisdom of supplying information to the people. The executive, moreover, has changed not only in its sheer size but in function as well, and by delegating to it rule-making powers and judicial powers, Congress has added reasons why the executive should be conducted more in conformity with the principles of disclosure that prevail, under law, in courts and in legislative establishments.

The reasons that argue for the fullest disclosure of the transactions and records of the executive departments often are more apparent in specific examples than in general terms. Yet it is possible to set down some principles to which administrators ought to advert before deciding to withhold information that it is within their discretion to conceal. Here are some of the reasons that are most apparent:

(1) Government is forever threatened by the danger that an abyss may appear between the governors and the governed. Policies of great merit will not preserve a government from

such a difficulty unless these policies are exposed to the day-to-day discussion and scrutiny of the people.

(2) The people will protect a government against the misfeasance or malfeasance of its own administrators if they are given sufficient access to the transactions of government so that they can detect improper conduct. They constitute the best 'inspector general' any central government ever had. Their omnipresent, omniscient, and incorruptible 'inspections' depend on their full information.

(3) Access of the public to the discussions and deliberations of administrative officers, while a program or a policy is under study, confer upon the executive the same advantages that the public presence at legislative proceedings confers upon Congress. If a proposal is a bad one, its weaknesses and flaws will emerge before it is put into effect. If it is a good one, the people, by their advance knowledge of it, will better understand the reasoning behind it, the need for it, the courses alternative to it, and will more cheerfully bear the burdens that it imposes.

(4) Officials of the executive department, like those in the courts, are, in the language of Bentham, 'kept up to the pitch of duty' by having their transactions and proceedings constantly under public scrutiny.

(5) The gulf between intent and performance menaces all central governments. The lag between the purpose of the government and the fulfillment of that purpose is likely to multiply with the size of a country and with the objects of government. The lag is most menacing in a country of continental distances and with a government of almost limitless function. If it is not to become so great that faulty performance in the field negates the purpose or even becomes policy, the people must be so adequately informed as to both purposes of government and field performance that central offices will feel quickly popular reaction to exaggerated lags.

(6) 'Public ingenuity,' as Jefferson describes it, will be enrolled in the solution of problems that face a regime if the people are given full information. It is important to notice here

that the government's failures to deal with a problem, frankly acknowledged, may invite even more 'public ingenuity' than reports of government success. Inversely, the suppression of information about these failures frequently may deprive the government of the benefit of suggestions and recommendations that frank acknowledgment of failure would elicit.

These general advantages of publicity sometimes seem insubstantial beside the particular advantages of official secrecy. The consequences of their disregard, unfortunately, are often deferred and cumulative rather than instant. They sometimes are outweighed in the minds of administrators by the instant pains and embarrassments of disclosure.

It is these pains, rather than formal interpretations of executive responsibility and authority, that account for the withholding of most information.

This is evident on examination of many of the disputes over access to information that have arisen in the past several years. An exception must be made of course for the cases involving military security, where certain special factors otherwhere absent influence decisions. The security cases will be dealt with in a separate chapter.

Many cases have arisen over operations involving the getting and spending of public funds. Control of the purse, historically, has been the most jealously guarded power of popular governments. Appropriation and taxing power, in almost all democratic governments, is in the popular branch of the legislature or parliament. Early English reformers rightly understood that in this power lay their best safeguard against the excesses of the executive. The power of the people's assembly to tax and to spend, however, cannot be maintained if the executive which operates under that power functions in secret so that neither citizens nor lawmakers may know if the taxes are being fixed in conformity with law or the appropriations made in fulfillment of the legislative prescription.

At local and state levels, generally, citizens may ascertain for themselves how uniformly and fairly taxes are being laid.

In many states, local governing bodies publish lists of taxpayers showing the amounts paid by each in personal property taxes and in real-estate taxes. In others, the information is available at county and local offices. The trend has been away from such publicity in the federal government. Pressures for privacy have prevailed over pressures for publicity. Income taxes, once public, now are confidential. Citizens may suspect discrimination or fraud but there is now no way they can quiet or confirm their suspicions. They must take for granted the honesty and fairness of the tax-gatherer. The tax return discloses so much about a citizen's business that a strong argument can be made for keeping it confidential. At the same time, it ought to be remembered that we have dispensed with a natural check on the tax-collector which our government, in the past, felt essential to maintain the integrity of the tax office.

Some governments still think so. The Norwegian 'Act on Taxation in the Cities,' in Section 79, provides that:

The taxation commission shall, upon completion of the tax assessments, display in one or more places and for public inspection a tax list, comprising all those obligated to pay taxes. The list shall further explain the rules according to which the assessments are calculated, the scale of reductions, the percentage used in calculating the taxes, the taxes thus calculated and the property, income and class on the basis of which the municipal and state tax of the taxable person has been calculated. The display of such lists shall be published in the ordinary manner.

The United States Treasury Department since 1953 has acknowledged that tax compromises and abatements ought to be made public and has agreed that there should be legislation on the subject, but legislation has not yet been approved.

Government expenditures also require closer public scrutiny than it is now possible to give them. There is some progress. The Jenner amendment finally permitted states to make relief rolls public, eliminating a danger of abuse from this quarter.

Until 3 December 1953, the Department of Agriculture, under the regulations of its Production and Marketing Division, forbade the publication of the names of those receiving drought aid. This made it impossible for local citizens to have any check on the field administration of the program. On 3 December the regulations were changed to 'permit a review of the records in the drought aid program at reasonable times.'

A Department of Agriculture circular issued 4 November 1953 forbade the release in the field of information on Agricultural Stabilization and Conservation Service loans. In January 1954, the policy was altered to allow field release of this information.

The Reconstruction Finance Corporation for many years operated under a policy by which information on loans to private persons and corporations was very much restricted. There is no doubt that the secrecy surrounding these transactions was partly to blame for some improper loans that came to light in congressional investigations in 1950–51. Subsequently the agency announced it was going to operate 'in a goldfish bowl.'

When the Agricultural Adjustment Administration was set up in 1933, it maintained secrecy on the adjustment payments and later soil conservation payments to individual farmers for a time. The secrecy finally was broken. Until the names and amounts were available it was not possible for citizens to make any intelligent appraisal of the program or to resolve the differences that had arisen over the proportionate attention being given to commercial farms and to family-sized farms.

The government payroll — and access to the names of those on it and the amount that they are paid — has been a subject of dispute since the beginning of the federal establishment.

The rule of publicity for the government payroll was introduced by Jefferson in his first annual message:

. . . we may well doubt whether our organization is not too complicated, too expensive; whether offices and officers have not been multiplied unnecessarily and sometimes injuriously to the service they were meant to promote. I will cause to be laid before you an essay toward a statement of those who, under public employment of various kinds, draw money from the Treasury or from our citizens.[6]

On 17 February 1802, a roster of federal officials and agents was delivered to Congress. In 1806, Congress required all the federal departments and offices to report the names of clerks employed year by year, and the sum given to each.[7]

The State Department in 1816 initiated *The Official Register*, a biennial compilation of all civil and military personnel.

In 1842 Congress extended the requirements for such publicity. It occasionally extended it to agencies and departments by specific enactment, applying it to each custom house in 1849 and to the Coast Survey in 1853. Leonard D. White, in his history of the Jacksonian period, observes:

> The rule of publicity was thus enforced on finance, contracts, and employment; and from time to time Congress required special reports on these and other phases of administrative operations. Each House of Congress also required its clerk to prepare annually a statement of all appropriations, a list of all new offices with the salaries of each, and a statement of all increases in salary.[8]

Congress was a long time in coming around to the same candor as to its own household that it required of the executive department. On 17 May 1932, Representative Lindsay C. Warren, of North Carolina, introduced a resolution opening the records of the House disbursing office to the public. It had the support of Speaker John Nance Garner who stated publicly: 'I approve of the resolution as I do not think there is any public business that should be private.' The resolution was passed on 20 May 1932, without objection. The Senate periodically publishes a list of its employees and their remuneration but does not make its records continuously available, as does the House.

Notwithstanding such precedents, old and modern, federal agencies from time to time still try to deny their payroll information to citizens.

The Public Housing Administration, on 28 May 1952, was asked for the names of those employed in its San Francisco-Oakland offices and declined to furnish them. Decisions of the regional office against disclosure, were supported in Washington by the PHA. Representations against disclosure were made by The American Federation of Government Employees, but in its statement the Federation objected to the use to which it alleged the *San Francisco Call-Bulletin* intended to put the sought-for information. James A. Campbell, the president of the employee organization, in a letter to the American Society of Newspaper Editors said: 'I believe the names and salaries of all government employees should be made available to any interested person at all times.'

The Commissioner of the Public Housing Administration on 12 August 1952 declined to release the names and salaries on the ground that he was not satisfied that the release would serve any 'useful public service.'

There the matter stood until 18 January 1955, when the Acting Commissioner of the Public Housing Administration, appealed to by the American Society of Newspaper Editors, wrote that the PHA had the feeling 'that as public servants our records should be available under any reasonable circumstances to anyone who has a legitimate use for them.'

The PHA, in this case, seems to reserve still the right to decide when circumstances are 'reasonable' or uses of names and salaries are 'legitimate.'

There is some room to doubt that such discretion ought to reside in an executive official in a democratic government. A citizen, one would think, would need no better credentials than his citizenship to entitle him to information of this kind. He who cannot discover who his governors are or how much of his tax money they are paid had better call himself a subject than style himself a citizen. Nor should a citizen be required to explain, to an administrator, before gaining access to payroll lists, whether he intends to use the information to praise or reproach the government. This seems to be an area in which express legislative requirements for publication of payrolls might be most useful.

One area of federal expenditure in which all information has been denied the public is that of congressional retirement payments. The rules provide that files and information 'will be deemed confidential and privileged, and no disclosure thereof will be made except as provided herein.' [9] The exceptions do not include disclosure to the general public.

This regulation throws the cloak of secrecy over the expenditure of millions of dollars of federal funds. It is possible to figure out, from the rates and salaries involved, what the retirement pay of an individual should be under the law. It is not possible to find out if any given individual is being paid more than he should receive. The public will have to take it for granted that there is no irregularity in the program, until the information policy is altered. This close secrecy is the more remarkable in view of the willingness of Congress to disclose the salaries of its own members while they are in the House or Senate.

The integrity of the government in financial affairs is one of the most important concerns of the public. Every aspect of money-getting and spending that can be divulged without jeopardy to security ought to be disclosed to the taxpayers who pay the bills. Because the government takes from and gives to millions of its own citizens, in transactions that would have been in the area of private business a generation ago, concepts of privacy and public concern sometimes come into conflict. Yet, all money transactions between the government and a citizen are of concern to a third party — the general public. Its rights in this area must be paramount.

If the executive department were entrusted only with the impartial administration of the laws that are passed by Congress, the public should have the most complete access compatible with security and efficient administration to all executive proceedings and records. This the people need to make sure that the law is being enforced without discrimination.

The executive department of the government of the United States is something infinitely more than the administrative agent of Congress. As more and more activities of American life engage the attention of Congress, that body is more and more frequently compelled to make sweeping delegations of power to the executive branch. The sheer press of legislative business requires Congress to content itself with staking out the broad purposes and outlines of policy under which the executive departments exercise wide discretion.

This process, in effect, delegates to executive departments some of the legislative power. Citizens need to have access to this rulemaking, lawmaking function, wherever it is exercised. Where the executive is permitted to take alternative courses to the same legislative end, citizens have a right to know the arguments for and against rival methods, just as they would have a right to hear the debates if Congress itself had picked the method in a statute. This is fine in theory, but in practice, many of the executive agencies that wield such essentially legislative powers habitually exercise them in secret. The advocates of alternative methods are not given public hearings. No citizen, prior to public announcement, knows what courses are advocated or who advocates them. The public often is confronted with a *fait accompli*.

This secret procedure is bad enough when the executive agents involved are the full-time, regularly appointed or elected, responsible officials of government. At least there is, in such cases, no doubt about the origins of the policy, and no concealment about the persons responsible for it. It is infinitely worse when executive departments make use of informal citizen advisory groups, as they do with increasing frequency. Slates of handpicked advisers, chosen by criteria not divulged to citizens, are summoned to Washington, impaneled in conference rooms, confronted with an executive dilemma, closeted off from the public, and required to produce a solution. No one hears their debates or discussion. They may proceed upon the most fallacious premises to the most illogical conclusions. No citizen ever knows. Their judgments may be biased and warped and far from disinterested. What personal, nongovernmental, profit considerations influence their conclusions no one can say. Perhaps they are unselfish and uniformly patriotic. No one can judge. They meet in secret. It often is argued that these worthy citizens would not speak frankly if their deliberations were in public. Perhaps they would not. Perhaps, sometimes, they might not wish to push private purposes in public, as they feel free to push them in secret sessions. They make recommendations that influence the lives and fortunes of citizens — and sometimes their own lives and their own fortunes. Sometimes their recommendations are disclosed. Sometimes they are not. In any case, a departmental decision emerges. If there are dissents in the policy committee, no one knows. If there is only imperfect agreement between the committee and the administrator, no one knows.

The advisory committee is a useful governmental device. It is a means of keeping bureaucratic administration in touch with practical reality. It is a method of enlisting the public ingenuity of which Jefferson was speaking in his message of 1801. It is a method which will work, however, without the prevailing secrecy in which these committees presently meet. As the delegation of rulemaking power in congressional enactments increases, and the reliance of executive agencies upon secret advisory committees to make the rules grows greater, the risk of a kind of secret legislative system becomes very real. It is a kind of secrecy that never would be tolerated in Congress or state legislatures, when exercised by duly elected representatives. It is much less to be tolerated when the secrecy is invoked by persons who never have been elected, who serve temporarily without the disciplines and restraints that professional governmental service imposes, and who are often virtually unknown to citizens.

At what point are citizens entitled to know about pending executive decisions? Obviously, in some cases, it is not proper for them to know of a government policy until its formal announcement. It is not feasible to reach, in public, some of the decisions the Federal Reserve Board must make, or some Treasury decisions, or crop market figures — or a host of other decisions of the kind.

In other areas, however, if public opinion is to have any influence on policy, citizens must be informed of alternative courses while executive deliberations are going on. Woodrow Wilson, for all his belief in full publicity, had a perfect horror of premature disclosure. Theodore Roosevelt, on the other hand, utilized the press to launch trial balloons that would invite public reaction while decisions were still pending. There are risks involved in making disclosure of tentative decisions. Whatever they are, however, they avoid the sometimes even more dangerous risk that a fully decided policy on its formal disclosure may be found to have fatal defects that inspire an embarrassing abandonment. The merest intimation that a given policy is under consideration may be sufficient to call forth from the public good reasons why the policy is not feasible.

## Mechanics of Disclosure

An American government that had decided to withhold from the American people none of its transactions, deliberations, or proceedings or records, would still face an enormous task in order to make effective the people's right to know.

Few citizens are situated so that they can have personal access to such information. It must reach most of them by formal announcement, periodic reports, informal statements to reporters of press and radio, direct use of press and radio in official statements, and by the formal press conference.

This involves the employment of a formal information apparatus, staff, and equipment through which officials can avail themselves of the media upon which citizens must rely for information. This is much criticized by some of the very people who utilize it most, including certain newspapers and politicians. This apparatus is as indispensable to the agencies putting out the information as it is to those receiving it. It can be dangerous if its purpose becomes pure propaganda or if it becomes a formidable barrier between the government and the people. It can be exceedingly useful, both in furnishing information executive agencies have decided to release, and in reminding them of their duty to furnish such information.

The official press conference, in the last twenty years, has become, in many ways, the most successful method of making available to the people the information about their own government in which they are chiefly interested. The presidential press conference has become much more than a means of disseminating information; it has become the informal counterpart of the question-and-answer period in the House of Commons. It has had a long historical development.

American Presidents from the beginning have acknowledged the importance of informing the public. George Washington, who was in some ways very suspicious of the press and reticent in his dealings with it, felt keenly the need for keeping the people informed. In his farewell address he said: 'In proportion as the structure of government gives force to public opinion it is essential that public opinion should be enlightened.'

In the last year of his life he wrote a letter urging efforts to inform the people and concluding with the sentence: 'Concealment is a species of misinformation; and misrepresentation and false alarms found the ground work of opposition.' [10]

James Monroe, in his seventh annual message, emphasized the point with this sentence: 'To the people every department of the Government and every individual in each are responsible, and the more full their information the better they can judge the wisdom of the policy pursued and the conduct of each in regard to it.'

Grover Cleveland, as President-elect, in February 1885, while on a visit to New York City to confer with party leaders, held daily press conferences with reporters and submitted to the kind of cross-examination common in these conferences today. He did not continue the practice in the White House, however, and his subsequent relations with the press were informal and generally unsatisfactory.[11]

William McKinley had his secretary confer with the press each night at about ten o'clock in a session which James E. Pollard, in his book on the Presidents and the press, believes had the 'real germ of the regular White House press conference.'

Theodore Roosevelt had more intimate associations with the press than his predecessors and saw news men frequently, but never countenanced anything like the open question-and-answer sessions later inaugurated.

Woodrow Wilson, at the very outset of his administration, arranged to see newspaper correspondents twice each week, inaugurating the modern press conference system. The experiment was relatively short-lived and was abandoned with the start of World War I.[12]

Warren Harding made the press conference a regular and permanent institution. After an erroneous oral reply to one question, Harding amended the Wilson method of impromptu questions and answers so as to provide for written questions, submitted in advance.[13]

Calvin Coolidge continued the press conference, but by the use of written questions and rejection of many of these he made the device much less useful than it was under Wilson and Harding.[14]

Herbert Hoover virtually abandoned the press conference during the closing months of his administration.

Franklin D. Roosevelt reinstituted the White House press conference as Wilson had originated it, divested it of the austerity and formality of the Wilson administration, and made it an instrument as efficient in communicating to the country an impression of the policies of government as the question period in the House of Commons.

Harry S. Truman continued the White House press conferences in the Roosevelt manner.

Following the election of Dwight D. Eisenhower there were reports that the President-elect disliked the White House press conference as a regular institution. It was said that he wished to hold the press conferences if, as, and when he had something to say and not periodically. When he assumed office, however, he instituted regular weekly press conferences. In February 1955, radio and television coverage was authorized for the first time.

From the standpoint of the public, the press conference has attributes possessed by no other device by which information can be gained about government personalities and policies. All other government-originated information deals with material which the government wishes to put out. It presents government policy as the government wishes it seen. Whatever its attribution, it may, in fact, be the product of anonymous authors. At the press conference, the public has an opportunity to seek what it wishes to know and is not limited solely to that which the government wishes to venture. The responses to questions illuminate not only policies but they divulge much about the policy-maker, too.

From the standpoint of the government, the press conference also has certain unique advantages over any other system for informing the public.

(1) It opens the front pages of American newspapers to government spokesmen.

(2) It provides, through the questions that are asked, information for the government, as well as eliciting, in the answers, information from the government.

(3) Its question and answer exchange is a psychologically sound method of presenting complicated government issues in understandable form.

(4) It permits the President, or other executives of an administration, to make disclosures in response to a question that

it might not be appropriate for the President or his associates to put out on their own initiative.

(5) It puts it within the power of an administration to fix the area of public discussion — either diverting it from a subject that it would prefer to defer or directing it to an issue that the administration wishes to exploit.

Departments of the federal government made the most effective use of the press conference in the first two Roosevelt administrations. After 1940 the press sessions of department heads were more irregular. The regular press conference is an institution in only a few of the Eisenhower departments. Most of the members of the Eisenhower cabinet prefer irregularly scheduled meetings with the press. Some of them hold hardly any such conferences at all — notably Secretary of Interior Douglas McKay.

Some cabinet officers feel as does Secretary McKay that the press conference is not necessary as long as individual reporters have ready access to them. These informal interviews, unfortunately, seldom furnish a chance for the department-wide survey of policies that only a general, open press conference can provide. Such informal conversations, in themselves, are a perfectly legitimate device for reaching the public with an official's point of view. They are essentially, however, a propaganda device — a means of putting out the information which the government wishes to disseminate, on the government's terms, in the official's own form. These meetings provide none of the question and answer, give and take that makes the open press conference illuminating and informative. The private interview is the device of the official. It is in the control of the man who gives the answers. The public press conference belongs to the people and is in the control of the men who ask the questions.

Less dramatic but probably more important than the press conference, in terms of the aggregate information forthcoming, is the day-to-day accessibility of lesser government officials. Where citizens are conceded the right to ask — and government officials allowed the right to answer — the people will be well informed about the operations of their government. Considerations of security and confidentiality have altered this once easy communication. The early officials of the government of the United States, as their correspondence attests, were not much inhibited in talking to friends and acquaintances about the duties that engaged them. The climate has changed. Several interludes of wartime secrecy, the various internal security programs, and the increasing number of government functions conducted in secret, have put a chill on this sort of ready and informal communication. Official frowns, and sometimes official punishments, have served to close up channels through which, at one time, much information flowed to the public.

In 1952, Secretary of War Robert Lovett referred to some talkative government workers as 'blabbermouths.' The Justice Department frequently has tried patiently to discover the source of information (however accurate) which emerged from other than official sources. The premature (prior to official release) disclosure of General Eisenhower's appointment to Supreme Allied Headquarters in Europe in 1950 precipitated an investigation of the leak by the Federal Bureau of Investigation. The dismissal of John Patton Davies by the State Department in 1954, connected as it was with the diplomat's conversations with newspapermen, could not fail to chill the inclination of foreign officers to be freely communicative.

New Mexico, in 1954, furnished a striking example of government reprisal against talking employees, at the state level. Victor E. Black, a teacher in the state reform school at Springer, New Mexico, on 23 November wrote a letter to the *New Mexican*, confirming stories it had printed about mistreatment of inmates by guards. On 25 November he was notified of his dismissal. Such lessons are not lost on other employees.

Government employees, of course, have a duty to respect the confidences acquired in the course of their services and to conform to laws and regulations imposing secrecy. In the area where policy and statutes permit discussion of their work, they ought to be free to discuss it with any citizens. And in cases of malfeasance or misfeasance in office, they have the same duty to their country that the laws and the instincts of patriotism impose upon all other citizens. Governments that invoke the power to punish or dismiss against employees who divulge that which the people have a right to know create the just suspicion of citizens. The people well may believe that secrecy, so enforced, is more for the convenience of the administration than for the good of the public.

Periodic reports of government agencies are a further source of information on the operation of executive departments. Since the start of World War II there has been a disposition, on the part of Congress, and on the part of government bureaus, to dispense with many such annual reports in the interests of economy. It is the feeling of the Second Hoover Commission that many such reports can be dispensed with. Former Representative John Hollister, executive officer of the Commission, addressing business editors of the country at a Washington meeting, indicated that the elimination of 'useless reports that gather dust on shelves and which no one reads' would be one purpose of the Commission. It is popular to refer to the 'paper flood' in Washington. The costs of some reports are considerable. It is a poor economy, however, which for the sake of a printing bill of a few hundred dollars withholds from the public the facts on government programs in which billions are being expended. To deprive the public of periodic reports of important agencies (each of which serves as a check on prior and on subsequent operations) is to obstruct an important flow of information.

It is not easy to prescribe, in complete detail and specifically, all the government information that should be divulged and all that properly may be withheld. It is possible to describe the spirit, the climate, the atmosphere that ought to pervade the government of a country that is democratically ruled. All the employees of government, elected and appointed, ought to be imbued with the feeling that the government does indeed belong to the people, who therefore have a right to know about all of its transactions, except for those expressly reserved to accredited persons by law or regulation.

The legitimate occasions for secrecy arising during two world wars and in a period of cold war; the sheer size of the federal government; the number of its activities which involve confidential relationships with citizens — all these circumstances have chilled the easy communicative nature once characteristic of the federal employee.

The inquiring citizen, at the threshold of the executive offices, in person or in the form of persons representing media on which the citizen depends, no longer is met by employees eager to explain what the government is doing and how it is doing it. He is likely to be asked why he wishes to know, or how he intends to use the information, or referred to printed releases. Government employees in the agencies dealing with the most routine civilian functions of government frequently give the impression of being on guard. The natural curiosity of citizens inspires suspicion. There is a chill in place of the easy accessibility of even twenty-five years ago.

The genuine wish of many officials to make the government responsive and communicative, of which the remarks of White House Assistant Sherman Adams at the Dartmouth Alumni meeting of 3 February 1954 are a sample, seems insufficient to melt this chill. Probably nothing can wholly dispel it as long as the present world situation persists. The impulse for secrecy is contagious. Each war renews the infection. Each crisis spreads it.

It is necessary now, as it may never have been necessary in the past, to spell out in the statutes provision for disclosure in the civilian operations of government. The Bureau of National Affairs, co-operating with the American Society of Newspaper Editors, commenced in January 1954 to examine all the bills introduced in Congress to see how many of them were deficient in this respect. It searched all legislation for measures that failed to provide for public access to records, periodic reports, open hearings, published regulations. It found hundreds of bills deficient. Congressional drafting clerks have been slow to develop standard clauses providing for access to operations of executive departments of the kind that have become standard in other areas. Hitherto, the public's right to know about the executive departments has been something that goes without saying. The late Carl Becker once said that we need to look at the things that go without saying once in awhile to see if they are still going. In this case, they aren't.

The process of legislating, bill by bill, for access to federal agencies, will be a slow and laborious one. It involves some risk; the absence of such specific terms may come to be interpreted as implying that in all such cases right of access does not exist. On the whole, however, it may be easier to do than it would be to pass a general access law, burdened with the inevitable exceptions.

The work of the Special Subcommittee on Government Information of the House Committee on Government Operations is a most encouraging augury of legislative remedy. On 1 November 1955, this committee published a report containing the replies of all government agencies to an extensive questionnaire on their policies and on the laws under which they claimed the right to withhold information.[15]

From 7 to 10 November the Subcommittee heard a succession of witnesses testify about various restrictions on information and also examined many department officials on their policies. The hearings resumed in January.

Two legislative changes seem plainly indicated. The 'housekeeping statute,' 5 U.S.C.A. 22, intended merely to authorize departments and agencies to take care of executive papers, has been stretched and construed into an authorization of secrecy and it ought to be brought back to its original meaning. The Administrative Procedures Act (5 U.S.C.A. 1001–11) which worked a great improvement needs to be amended to make it even clearer that the proceedings opened up to litigants and counsel are also open to the public.

The report of 1 November (and subsequent hearings) point to a host of other particular enactments that need clarifying so as to prevent the withholding of matter to which the public ought to have access.

It will take a great many years to put a proper statutory foundation under the people's right to know about the executive departments of their government. Congress finally has made a tardy beginning by the selection of the Moss subcommittee.

# 4

---

## THE RIGHT TO KNOW ABOUT THE
## MILITARY ESTABLISHMENT

*Your fellow citizens think they have a right to full
information, in a case of such great concernment to
them. It is their sweat which is to earn all the expenses
of the war, and their blood which is to flow in expiation
of the causes of it.* — THOMAS JEFFERSON *

THE operations of the military establishment of the government of the United States include the transactions upon which
the nation's survival most depends, on which three fourths of
all our expenditures are made, and in which three fourths of
all persons employed by government are engaged.

Yet, the citizens in whose behalf and at whose expense all
these exertions are made know little about them. They do not
know enough to judge the wisdom of the expenditures approved by Congress or the necessity for the taxes levied to
sustain these appropriations. They do not know enough to

* Letter to Elbridge Gerry, 26 January 1799, *The Writings of
Thomas Jefferson*, Thomas Jefferson Memorial Association, Washington, 1904, vol. X, p. 83.

judge of the efficiency, or even honesty, of the civilian administrators who have authority over hundreds of thousands of employees and billions of dollars in public funds. They do not know enough to estimate the training, ability, judgment, or genius of the military commanders into whose hands they have put the lives of their sons, the great part of their fortunes, and the military destiny of the nation.

This has happened in a country once so distrustful of military establishments that the existence of a standing army was viewed with distrust and anxiety and opposed as a public policy. This has happened in a country where secrecy in any government activity once was widely reprobated and in a military organization especially deplored.

It has come about, not by anyone's deliberate design or calculated conspiracy, but as the result of fell circumstance. It exists because a world in chaos, and in imminent threat of destruction, has imposed upon government and citizens disciplines to which they never would otherwise consent. These disciplines and restraints deprive the citizens of the benefits of information and they divest the government of the advantages that spring from the constant scrutiny and the freest criticism of all governmental activity.

Americans hitherto have submitted to such restrictions upon their freedom for intervals of war. They have had the comfort of the knowledge that the end of the wars would end the restraints. They enter upon this abandonment of right now with no such assurance. Powers and privileges that no American government in peacetime hitherto would have dared ask an electorate to resign for the very shortest period are being given up for a time without limit. No man can say when this crisis will end. No man dare hope that those now living will outlast it. Powers given up for years, for decades, or even for a generation may be regained. The recollection of better and freer days keeps alive through short interludes of deprivation the memory of freedoms resigned but still remembered. Powers given up for several generations — or even centuries — are not likely ever to be restored. And if they are powers so great and so essential that their denial constitutes in fact an alteration of the system of government, it is reasonable to assume that institutions so long bent to a special purpose will not recover their former shape when the purpose itself has been abandoned.

Proposals for secrecy now must be examined in the light of these perspectives. It certainly would be unwise, in these altered circumstances, to abandon any of the precautions imposed to guard against the abuse of wartime censorship; and logically, we ought to strengthen these precautions in the face of secrecy that is bound to pervade our society more completely and certain to last longer than any period of secrecy that has preceded it.

It must be acknowledged that the freest governments in the world have found it necessary to impose secrecy on military operations in wartime. Where they have failed to do so, lives of citizens have been the price exacted. An admiralty agent of the British government was summarily executed in France in 1697 after the *London Gazette* printed information he had obtained.[1] British censorship at other times was close and extreme. In 1649, an Act of Parliament provided that the Secretary of the Army would be empowered to license all army news.[2]

Colonial governments frequently resorted to censorship in wartime. Typical of such precautions was a Massachusetts Order-in-Council of 13 May 1725, declaring that 'the printers of the newspapers in Boston be ordered upon their peril not to insert in their prints anything of the public affairs of this province relative to the war without the order of the government.' [3]

The American government, during the Revolutionary War, made ineffectual efforts at secrecy but was patient under dangerous disclosures and opposed in principle to concealment of some kinds. Thomas Jefferson, in a letter written in 1813, recalled: 'The first misfortune of the Revolutionary war induced a motion to suppress or garble the account of it. It was rejected with indignation.' [4]

During the American Civil War, secrecy precautions fluctuated wildly. Sometimes Washington and military commands in the field leaked information like sieves. Other times, the government took extreme measures to preserve secrecy. The Civil War experience offered bad instruction in both the dangers of disclosure and the evils of secrecy. The *Chicago Times* was suppressed by a military order. The *New York World* and the *New York Journal of Commerce* were temporarily suppressed for printing a forged presidential order, known as the 'gloomy proclamation.' Many newspapers were denied mailing privileges. The *Washington Sunday Chronicle* was seized for disclosing troop movements. General Ambrose E. Burnside, commander of the Department of Ohio, attempted to close the *Chicago Times* on 3 June 1863. Severity alternated with amazingly lax security precautions under which reporters were allowed access to military secrets.

The Spanish-American War saw little effort at maintaining military secrecy and the only notable incident concerned Signal Corps handling of access to cables.

The Mexican disputes of 1914 saw some naval censorship at Vera Cruz, but ordinary peacetime conditions prevailed generally inside the country.

Censorship in World War I commenced on 24 March 1917 with the promulgation of a set of regulations by the State, War, and Navy Departments. Newspapers were asked to adhere to them voluntarily. One of them requested that 'no information, reports, or rumors, attributing a policy to the government in any international situation, not authorized by the President or a member of the cabinet, be published without first consulting the Department of State.' On 14 April 1917, President Wilson created the Committee on Public Information and World War I censorship got under way. The administrator of the program, George Creel, thought that the censorship was unworkable. He found the whole effort of a piece with 'the hysterical "shush-shushing" that warned against unguarded speech, just as though every citizen possessed some important military secret.' He said, at the end of the war, 'virtually everything we asked the press not to print was seen or known by thousands.' He believed the answer to be 'secrecy at the source' through the military departments.

In World War II, a much more efficient and effective system of voluntary censorship was employed. It was a system that profited by the mistakes of World War I. It separated propaganda and censorship and, in effect, supported by voluntary agreement the withholding of information which the armed forces thought it dangerous to disclose. It was, in reality, a system for making effective the sort of censorship at the sources of information that Creel had talked about at the end of World War I.

The first formal effort to withhold information in the World War II period came on 31 December 1940 when Secretary of Navy Frank Knox asked 5000 radio, news, and picture editors to avoid any mention of:

(1) Actual or intended movements of vessels or aircraft of the United States Navy, of units of naval enlisted personnel or divisions of mobilized reserves, or troop movements of the United States Marine Corps.

(2) New United States Navy ships or aircraft.

(3) United States Navy construction projects ashore.

Communications media generally co-operated. They were reproached for reporting congressional discussions of Navy movements and for disclosing the presence in the United States of the British warship *Malaya*.

As the situation tightened there were other requests for the voluntary suppression of news of military importance, including weather bureau requests for restricted handling of weather news. In August of 1941, Chairman James L. Fly of the Communications Commission urged a conference of media representatives not to build up a legend that the 'Stalin Line' was invincible, but his 'advice' was not taken seriously.

In September, the War and Navy Departments disclosed they were making plans for censorship of all outgoing communications.

On the declaration of war, on 8 December, censorship was put into effect. J. Edgar Hoover was made temporary co-ordinator of all news and communications censorship. The President appealed to press and radio to refrain from the publication of unconfirmed reports. The Navy announced the censorship of outgoing communications. Chairman Emory S. Land asked media to refrain from giving out information on the movement of commercial shipping. The Navy put out a statement calling attention to the reimposition of the provisions of the Espionage Act of 1918 and appealed for adherence to the regulations of 31 December 1940. The War Department restricted information on routes, schedules, and destination of troop movements. The Office of the Coordinator of Information took charge of outgoing short-wave broadcasts. The Weather Bureau restricted its reports. Then, on 16 December, President Roosevelt announced the appointment of Byron Price, formerly executive news editor of the Associated Press, as Director of Censorship.

The announcement said that:

(1) It was necessary to withhold some news at its source.

(2) It was necessary to set a watch upon the nation's borders so no information might reach the enemy.

(3) It was necessary to prohibit domestic publication of some types of information.

(4) The government was requesting the press and radio to abstain voluntarily from dissemination of detailed information of certain kinds, such as reports of the movement of vessels and troops.

On 19 December, the President formally created the Office of Censorship, under Section 303, Title III of the Act of 18 December 1941, Public Law 354, 77th Congress, First Session. This formal order empowered the director:

. . . in his absolute discretion to censor communications by mail, cable, radio or other means of transmission, passing between the

United States and any foreign country, or which may be carried by any vessel or other means of transportation touching at any port, place or territory of the United States and bound to or from any foreign country, in accordance with rules and regulations as the President shall from time to time prescribe.

The first code of wartime practices for newspapers, magazines, and other periodicals was issued on 15 January 1942 and wartime censorship was formally launched. The code was revised each six months. It described categories of news that were not to be published without appropriate authority, listing in seventeen different clauses information that required authorization before publication.

These included troop strengths and movement, ship movements, ship sinkings, air attacks, disposition of aircraft, descriptions of fortifications, production contracts and capacity, weather forecasts and reports, rumors on enemy damage, photographs and maps useful to the enemy, and reports of casualties.

The significant words in the operation of the code were 'appropriate authority.' The Office of Censorship did not undertake to suppress information that 'appropriate authority' officially gave out.

At the end of the war, Director Byron Price summarized the principles upon which the censorship had been conducted. He said:

(1) Voluntary censorship must deal only with questions involving security.

(2) It must never base a request on any security consideration which may be questionable. The danger to security must be real, and must be backed by a solid and reasonable explanation.

(3) It must avoid any interference whatever with editorial opinion. Such opinion could not possibly be controlled on a voluntary basis, even if it were desirable.

(4) It must never be influenced by non-security considerations of policy or public needs. Any involvement in these fields would destroy effectiveness elsewhere.

(5) It must make no requests which would put the press in the

position of policing or withholding from publication the utterances of responsible public officials.

(6) It must make every effort to avoid multiple censorship and on no account must withhold from the American public any information which has been generally disseminated abroad.

(7) It must never undertake to vouch for the truth or accuracy of any news story. The embarrassments would be too great for a voluntary system, based on security, to survive.

(8) It must never undertake to regulate release dates or other matters of newspaper ethics. To do so would encourage Government interference of a considerable and possibly uncontrollable character.

(9) It must be absolutely impartial and consistent. If any censor is to maintain a position of influence, his blue pencil must know no brother among competitors.

(10) It must operate openly, advising the public of every request made of the press. To do otherwise would undermine public confidence and foster unwarranted suspicion both against the Government and the press.

The Office of Censorship was terminated on 15 August 1945.

Communications media were thenceforth free to print or relate that which they possessed of their own immediate knowledge or information, and such 'censorship' as existed thereafter consisted of censorship at the source through the power of the government to withhold information in its control.

The defense establishment and agencies of government dealing with military information continued to employ security designations of 'Top Secret,' 'Secret,' 'Confidential,' and 'Restricted' for material not to be disclosed except to accredited persons in the government.

A special act of Congress covered the withholding of information on atomic secrets.

Field censorship methods used during the war, of course, are always available to armed forces wherever they may be actually engaged within a combat theater. These powers continued to be invoked in modified form when troops were engaged in occupation duties.

Government continued to possess formidable authority for withholding information about the military establishment which it did not wish to have disclosed.

As the behavior of Soviet Russia caused more and more alarm and tension in world affairs, officials of the government, from time to time, expressed the desire for additional restraints upon the free flow of information about the military departments themselves and about technical information of various kinds that might be useful to an enemy.

In the fall of 1947, the Security Advisory Board of the State Department-Army-Navy-Air Force Co-ordinating Committee proposed a new system of classification which it wished to use to ban, among other things, information that might cause 'serious administrative embarrassment.' It included also information which would cause 'unwarranted injury to an individual.' A dispute over such definitions of 'classified information' put an end to these proposals for a time.

In March 1948, Secretary of Defense James Forrestal tried to tighten up security information. He called a meeting of representatives of various communications media. He told them, on 3 March 1948, that he saw the problem in two major aspects, involving:

(1) Remedial action within the military establishment in regard to the prevention of 'leaks,' the declassification of documents whose security no longer obtains, and the establishment of a unified policy among the various armed services for the prompt release of technical information which does not endanger national security.

(2) An assumption by the information media of their responsibility in voluntarily refraining from publishing information detrimental to our national security.

The Secretary proposed a 'security advisory council' of six members, appointed from the media ranks, to advise the Secretary, and an information advisory unit within the military establishment to answer inquiries on certain security subjects and offer guidance to the news media.

This proposal never was put into effect.

Subsequently, the Secretary of Commerce, Charles Sawyer, made a gesture in the same direction. His proposals also proved generally unacceptable, and were dropped.

On 25 September 1951, President Harry Truman approved Executive Order 10-290, to tighten up on security controls. The White House had conferred briefly on the order with a special committee of the American Society of Newspaper Editors, headed by its president, Alexander F. Jones. This group opposed the order. Nevertheless, the National Security Council went ahead and approved it on 12 July and it was promulgated on 25 September.

This order authorized the agencies of government to employ the 'Top Secret,' 'Secret,' 'Confidential,' and 'Restricted' designations on material. It empowered heads of agencies to designate persons in the agencies authorized to classify information. It avoided the earlier disputes over definition of the classifications by using the vaguest language in describing them.

It was opposed at once by media groups for extending to nonmilitary agencies the use of the secret classifications, for failure to define closely the different categories of secret information, for investing agency heads with power to delegate classifying responsibilities, for absence of any adequate system under which the decisions of classifying officers could be reviewed, and for failure to provide any appeal from the decisions of the classifying agencies.

In making the order known, President Truman enjoined government officials not to abuse these powers and use them to cover mistakes or embarrassments, and he promised that his own press relations office would handle any complaints of overclassification or abuse of powers.

These assurances did not satisfy critics of the order and it was under continuous attack.

On 6 November 1953, President Dwight D. Eisenhower announced the substitution of a new order (10-501) for the Truman order. The new order limited the number of agencies that may use classification powers, restricted the authority of agency heads to delegate this responsibility, more clearly defined the security classifications, eliminated the classification 'Restricted' altogether, and made more definite provision for appeal and review. Classification powers were withdrawn altogether from twenty-eight agencies and its use limited in seventeen agencies.

In releasing the text of the order, the White House issued a statement saying: 'Throughout the lengthy consideration of this order it has been the purpose to attain in it the proper balance between the need to protect information important to the defense of the United States and the need for citizens of this democracy to know what their government is doing.'

Far less objectionable than the order which preceded it, the new executive order still is open to some criticism. The most serious of these is its failure to provide for an adequate weighing of the needs of security and information at the time of classification, and its failure to set up an adequate system of appeal to which the decisions of an agency to classify can be taken for a further review. It is said in its defense, as it was said in defense of the prior order, that complaints have been few. Since only those in favor of an act of classification have knowledge of what has been classified, it is not remarkable that outsiders have discovered few examples in which power has been abused.

On 5 November 1954, the government turned again to the field which Secretary Forrestal and Secretary Sawyer had explored. Secretary of Commerce Sinclair Weeks announced that at the direction of the President and on the recommendation of the National Security Council, he was setting up an Office of Strategic Information in the Department of Commerce. This office, he said, would provide a central location within the Government which would work with the business community 'in voluntary efforts to prevent unclassified strategic data from being made available to those foreign nations which might use such data in a manner harmful to the defense interests of the United States.'

In a statement on 3 January 1955, the director of the new agency, R. Karl Honaman, described the OSI as 'a small, fact-finding policy recommending group in the Department of Commerce' set up to 'cooperate with the publishing world, industrial community and Federal agencies.'

The Office, he said, was concerned 'only with the kinds of information and "know how" a potential enemy could use to injure us, yet which cannot be properly handled by classification.'

In the case of some highly specialized information, Mr. Honaman thought that a relatively small number of people really needing the information could be given it easily through specific channels 'without the need to broadcast it to nations whose interests are inimical to our own.'

The Honaman announcements were not well received by the general press, by the technical publications chiefly affected, or by newspaper societies. The new project was criticized for:

(1) Adding a new classification over which the government is to exert control, in addition to 'Top Secret,' 'Secret,' and 'Confidential.'

(2) Failing to define 'strategic information' in a clear-cut way that would limit the operations of the agency.

(3) Employing discrimination against some companies and partiality to others (who are to get needed information) with the giving and withholding of such favor at government discretion, under no published system of rules and regulations.

(4) The inference that a system of information control is not censorship if it is voluntary, when the censorship methods of two world wars were voluntary — but nonetheless censorship.

The new proposals seem to have been made without much regard for many of the parting points made by the administrator of World War II censorship, particularly because:

(1) Contrary to Byron Price's point two, the plan is to operate with reference to requests where the security consideration is 'questionable.'

(2) Without regard to Price's suggestion that censorship should not regulate release dates, it apparently contemplates the regulation of the time of publication for much technical data.

(3) In disregard of Price's point nine contention that the censorship must at all odds be 'absolutely impartial and consistent,' a discriminating and inconsistent withholding and disclosure is suggested.

(4) Far from operating openly and advising the public of every request made to the press (as Byron Price urges in his tenth point), it inclines toward a confidential and private operation, and a personal relation with individual editors.

If the OSI is successful at all in diminishing the flow of information, as it relates to technical data not covered by classification, it is difficult to see how it can avoid cutting down on the information reaching the American people. And if it cuts down on the amount of such information going to American citizens, it is difficult to see how it can avoid interference with industrial progress. One of the things that has accounted for American technical progress surely has been the facility and speed with which a new departure, a novel method, in one plant becomes industry-wide in its application. Heretofore, the American impulse has been to speed the circulation of such knowledge by every known means — by word of mouth, by trade associations, by technical publications, and by general broadcast. Sometimes, knowledge of this sort of 'know how' has sped all too swiftly to suit management in an individual plant. The impulse to share private discoveries sometimes has been too strong to be overcome by private advantage. It seems most likely that a prolonged effort to intercept and discourage this kind of exchange, even in the interest of checking the advantage it gives other powers, may alter profoundly the character of American enterprise.

The degree to which industrial secrecy can impair the productivity of a country and the defense of a nation is dramatically disclosed in Marc Bloch's *L'Étrange Defaite*, quoted in Herbert Luethy's *France against Herself*. In discussing the weaknesses of prewar France, as analyzed by Bloch, Luethy writes:

The grotesque inadequacy of her [France's] statistics, which differentiated France from all other civilized countries, the *stuffy secrecy of her industry* [my italics], which felt most at home in the semiobscurity of *les petites affaires*, was matched by the inadequacy of the chief organs of public information. . .[5]

Efforts of the military establishments to maintain photographic security have been the cause of frequent difficulty. Military guards often have interfered with photographers attempting to take photographs of air crashes and other accidents involving military equipment. The regulations of the three services by the end of 1954 prescribed procedures at the scene of accidents which, if followed, would avoid such military interference with civilian personnel.

Navy personnel are told that in the event of possible compromise of military security through civilian photography, outside military jurisdiction, they are to warn photographers of the classified nature of subject matter and request that pictures not be taken, or, if taken, the unexposed film be turned over to the military authority. The regulations state: 'Under no circumstances shall naval personnel use any degree of force to prevent or otherwise interfere with civilian photographers obtaining pictures outside of naval jurisdiction.' [6]

Photographic policy is governed by Special Regulation No. 360-5-15 of the United States Army. It provides that military personnel will withhold consent to take photographs until they can determine if classified material is exposed to view; that they will remove it or cover it if this is the case; and that consent to take photographs will be given if no classified material is visible. Army personnel are directed to inform photographers that it is unlawful to photograph classified material. If photographers persist, military personnel will ask for the plates or film, and warn that keeping them is a law violation. They are to ask for aid of local peace officers and report to their commanding officer in case of further refusal.

The United States Air Force similarly defines procedure, and provides that (1) consent will be withheld until presence or absence of classified material is ascertained; (2) it will be covered or removed; (3) if it cannot be covered or removed photographers will be warned; (4) plates will be asked for if pictures are taken; (5) help of civilian officers will be sought if delivery is refused.[7]

The regulations of all the services seek to avoid the physical interference of military personnel with civilian activities, and to leave the enforcement of the law against civilians to local peace officers or to the Federal Bureau of Investigation.

For many years, the armed forces refused to divulge the names of military personnel involved in accidents, on or outside of military installations, until next of kin were notified. This often involved delays of many hours. The exact lapsed time was altered now and then, fluctuating between four hours and twelve hours, outside the combat theaters.

This led to a great deal of confusion and distress. It was confusing to communication media because the military used, for mere policy reasons in the zone of the interior, an authority essential in the combat areas for security reasons.

It was distressing to the relatives of military personnel because it often left them uncertain as to the fate of their relatives hours after military accidents.

An overturned shore boat during a Mediterranean cruise a few years ago killed the shore party members. Their names were held up pending notification of their relatives. Meanwhile, the news of the accident was published everywhere in the United States. More than 2000 anxious relatives sent telegrams to the Navy Department to find out if sons or brothers were involved. Nonetheless the names of those drowned were held up, pending notification of relatives.

Parents and other relatives of thousands of draftees on a New Jersey post were similarly upset in 1952. An aircraft crashed into a truck and killed and injured many of the occupants in a mishap at Camp Kilmer. Names of the casualties were withheld pending notification, and in the interval of delay thousands of parents had to wait and wonder if their own sons were involved.

The policy was carried to a ridiculous extreme in May 1952. Two automobiles crashed head-on near Cheyenne, Wyoming, on 4 May. In one was Airman Third Class Ernest A. Laramee. He was accompanied by his wife. He was killed instantly and his wife died in a Cheyenne hospital three hours later. The wife's name was released to the press but the airman's name, under next-of-kin rules, was held up. Names were used anyway. The Air Force public-relations officers objected. They thought the press should have said, 'an unidentified airman.' Newspapers protested they could not report that Mrs. Laramee was killed while riding in a car with an unidentified airman.

On 22 October 1952, the Defense Establishment issued a directive modifying the next-of-kin rules of all the services. It provides that in case of accidents on posts and stations, names may be withheld until next-of-kin can reasonably be expected to have received notification but 'every effort should be made to release such names simultaneously with, or as soon thereafter as possible, the release of the accident news itself, so as to remove or lessen the anxiety of relatives of other personnel on the installation." In case of accidents outside posts and stations, names of military personnel are to be released on identification unless the event takes place in remote wilderness areas, in which case post rules will apply.

The new rules have not eliminated all difficulty. On the night of 8 April 1956, six marine recruits at Parris Island lost their lives in a training exercise. News that they had been drowned was released Monday morning and published in afternoon newspapers of 9 April. Relatives of some of the casualties received telegraphic notice by nine o'clock that night. Names were not made public until twelve-thirty a.m., 10 April. Newspaper offices throughout the country received the frantic requests of parents of the more than 7000 recruits on the base trying to find out if their sons were involved. The delay was in part excused by the problems of identification but the release was not as prompt as that envisioned in the Defense Department directive.

Both the photographic and the next-of-kin rules illustrate how precautions initially taken in the interest of security come to be applied as a matter of policy where no considerations of security are involved. There is not much argument about the risks of photographs of classified material; but many a civilian photographer has been physically interfered with while trying to take a picture of a plane that hasn't been classified for ten years. There is not much controversy over the security need of holding up all casualty information from a combat area, but the military secrecy so long practiced in reference to the victims of accidents in this country, even on public streets and highways, was inexcusable.

The habit of secrecy, warranted under combat conditions, seems to fasten its lifelong infection upon some military personnel. It is doubly unfortunate. It deprives citizens of information to which they are entitled. And it conditions them to look with suspicion and distrust upon requests for secrecy that are justified by the demands of security.

One of the stated purposes of Executive Order 10-501, setting up the security classifications for material of military importance, was to confine withholding of information to information properly classified as 'Secret,' 'Top Secret,' or 'Confidential.'

The promulgation of this order in 1953 has been followed, however, by the introduction of various processes and procedures for withholding information that is not classified at all.

On 29 March 1955, Secretary of Defense Charles E. Wilson issued a directive instructing officials of the Defense Establishment to confine their information activities to work that would make a 'constructive contribution' to the mission of the Department. When it was protested that it is for citizens, and not for the government, to decide whether or not information is 'constructive,' conferences looking to the amendment of the directive were held. Subsequently, the Department took the position that the directive applied to information being initiated by the Department and not to that given in response to requests.

R. Karl Honaman, Deputy Assistant Defense Secretary in Charge of Public Affairs, on 17 June, in a letter to the Freedom of Information Committee of The American Society of Newspaper Editors, said:

The public are eager to be informed of the activities of the Defense Department and need to have this information in order to play their part effectively as citizens. There are, nevertheless, many cases where demands for information which take up the time of people with busy schedules do not truly meet the requirement of being useful or valuable, nor yet very interesting to the public. These are tests that should be met. Thus, I would substitute for self-serving, public-serving, and I am sure this is a part of the interpretation of constructive.

Newspapers objected to this interpretation of the order and asserted it was up to the press and to the public to decide what is 'interesting' and 'useful.'

On 21 June, Honaman, in an interview with the United Press, voiced the hope that newspapers would voluntarily refrain from publishing information that is not secret, but might prove helpful to the Russians. He called this 'grey area' information.

This request was widely criticized as a threat to the circulation of the sort of technical information on which the country's technological progress heretofore has depended and as an invitation to the press to operate a censorship that would deprive citizens of information needed to make sound judgments on defense policy.

On 15 September 1955, the Federal Register published another Defense Establishment directive, in the form of instructions sent to private defense contractors. 'In such a manner,' the contractors were told 'publication of that segment of information of possible use to a potential enemy can be prevented.'

This standard (of possible use to a potential enemy) was criticized by the Freedom of Information Committee as really no standard or limit at all inasmuch as, it was argued, all information of any kind is of some possible use to a potential enemy. Critics pointed out that even though useful to an enemy in some small degree, much information about production, highways, weather, and other aspects of daily life must nevertheless be given the American public because of its much greater importance to them.

The Defense Establishment defended this document as only a 'recommendation' to private contractors and not an 'order,' but editors protested that defense suppliers would be much inclined to regard the department's suggestions and recommendations as 'orders.'

The Associated Press Managing Editors Association, at its meeting in Colorado Springs in November 1955, adopted a resolution stating:

The association expressly condemns the withholding of information that has not been classified and that is not eligible for classifying on the pretext that it is not 'constructive' or on the excuse that even though it is nonsecurity information it might be of 'possible use' to a potential enemy.

The need for military secrecy in the sort of world in which we now exist is self-evident. The dangers of extending secrecy beyond military security ought to be equally self-evident. The dangers of even military secrecy, strictly confined to matters of security, may be greater than we have anticipated. They have begun to alarm citizens most familiar with these restrictions and with their consequences.

Dr. Lloyd V. Berkner, president of Associated Universities, Inc., has repeatedly pointed out these dangers.

One can readily understand the need for security with respect to a specific weapon, where disclosure would not only permit its duplication but would also render it susceptible to enemy counter-measures. But the present craze for secrecy goes far beyond this. It is bad enough to deny to our own people information that is already in the hands, not only of friendly nations, but of those behind the Iron Curtain as well. It is outrageous to cover inaction and weakness by secrecy when disclosure would lead to public support of remedial measures. I view the mania for secrecy not simply as a danger to academic freedom, but as a national infection that is sapping our strength by concealing second-rate administration; by permitting unjustified rationalization of our national strength; by preventing the discussion with our allies of vital problems; by denying us the safeguards of swift progress that go with freedom of information; by subtly introducing government control of new processes and thereby undermining our system of free enterprise; and above all, by creating artificial barriers among men that stimulate the feelings of mistrust and hatred among men that are the seeds of war. We want no iron curtain here in America. The protection of our whole democratic system, of which academic freedom is but a part, calls for a searching inquiry into this creeping infection and measures for its prompt control.[8]

In another address Dr. Berkner has undertaken to outline the desirable limits on technological secrecy. He thus summarizes them:

1. In a democracy it is absolutely impossible to cloak a large undertaking in full security. . .
2. Widespread security of technological information is inimical to the security of progress, which is based on well-developed weapons and men trained to use them effectively. In the absence of an Iron Curtain, security of information must depend on compartmentalization of knowledge. Very little compartmentalization is needed to destroy scientific progress or to restrict training and limit tactical familiarity with weapons. Therefore, if we are to have security based on progress, the information to be restricted must be sharply defined. If, eventually, we should have to fight, we must decide now whether it is to be with effective weapons about which

an enemy knows a great deal or with pieces of paper about which
he knows nothing.

3. The regulations necessary to the maintenance of secrecy in large
areas of technological information condition the scientist to avoid
the conception of militarily valuable ideas. . . Excessive security
prevents some of the world's most creative men from contributing
to our national welfare.

4. The secrecy of technological information is incompatible with
the public policy function of a democracy. In our elective system
there is no certainty that policy-making officials will possess the
competence required for wise decisions or even understand what
elements of information are important . . . sound policy results
from the careful examination of the facts by the people of our nation and depends upon their diverse training and interests. Secrecy
prevents the discussion necessary to such examination, and compartmentalization prevents proper evaluation even by trained special-
ists. . .

5. Widespread secrecy of technological information keeps the
public ignorant of the adjustments it must make in the face of technological change. . .

6. Widespread technological secrecy with respect to national ca-
pabilities may lead the enemy to underestimate our power, and encourage him in irresponsible adventures leading to war.

Berkner and many others believe that a deep and searching
inquiry into the virtues of secrecy now is in order. We have
accepted unquestioningly the proposition that some secrecy is
essential to our security and our survival; but on sober second
thought it is possible to see many situations in which secrecy
not only has menaced our democratic institutions but in
which it has imperiled the very security it was supposed to
defend.

The doubts about it surely are sufficient to justify the acceptance of the principle that there are two sides to the
issue of secrecy — just as there are to most other policies —
even though we have been behaving as though there were only
one side.

We need to take a hard look at the dangers of disclosure.

We need to take a hard look at the dangers of secrecy.

We need to decide which menaces us most, in each instance

where secrecy is sought. We need to make an effort at compromise, so far as the two considerations are at all compatible.
We have been so preoccupied with the requirements of secrecy
that we have put all the penalties of the law, all the coercion of
opinion, all the impact of regulation on the side of secrecy.
We have many a penalty, legal and social, for those who do not
practice enough secrecy. We have no penalties at all for those
who practice too much secrecy.

Yet the risks of too much secrecy, as we have seen, are very
great:

(1) It threatens democratic government, which depends on
full information.

(2) It threatens scientific progress, which relies upon the
use of all knowledge.

(3) It threatens to divide the nation into an informed elite
(in terms of defense) and an ignorant mass.

(4) It threatens the efficiency of officials who are relieved
of the prod of public knowledge, the spur of public criticism,
and the aid of public suggestion.

(5) It may so well conceal our prowess at arms from an
enemy as to encourage him to believe he may insult us with
impunity.

This is, in fact, if not in law, a time of war, and many of the
restrictions to which American citizens cheerfully submitted
in World War II may have to be imposed again. Yet, they
ought not be submitted to blindly.

Citizens cannot be deprived of all information that might be
of use to an enemy and be well enough informed to continue a democratic government. All information is of some
use to an enemy. Not all of it can be kept secret. It might help
to decide what can be kept secret if we ranged all information
in categories of a different sort than those conventionally discussed, such as:

(1) Information of so little use to an enemy that secrecy
would be without purpose.

(2) Information of some use to an enemy, but of so much

use to American citizens, in the conduct of private business and the discharge of the duties of citizenship, that it would hurt us more to keep it secret than it would help an enemy to make it public. This would include statistics on agricultural and industrial production, maps of cities and harbors, transportation schedules, weather forecasts, etc.

(3) Information of substantial value to an enemy but which is of even greater value to citizens, so that secrecy with respect to it would work great hardship on us while working lesser hardship on a foe. This would include much of the so-called strategic information necessary for the progress of science and industry.

(4) Information of enormous value to an enemy but which also is of enormous value to Americans. This is the area of greatest difficulty, in which the right to know must be weighed constantly against the duty to conceal. Definitions are difficult and standards troublesome. Decisions ought to be made with both security and information requirements in mind.

(5) Information of decisive military value to an enemy. Secrecy here would be the rule, as long as it really served the purpose of enemy denial.

Even with such a philosophy of secrecy, difficulties will be great — particularly where the last two categories are concerned. Such a philosophy would at least have the merit of linking together for simultaneous consideration the reasons for secrecy and the reasons for disclosure.

Our present methods are depriving citizens of information they require to fulfill their role in a democratic government. They are even depriving Congress of the military information it needs to perform its constitutional duties. As the Committee on Economic Development has pointed out:

Everyone would admit that security consideration should impose limits on the extent of public information. There is considerable likelihood, however, that the Congress may be less well informed than the enemy. . . The principle of parity with the enemy should be accepted as a minimum criterion for the information to which Congress as a whole and the public are entitled.[9]

Acknowledging the need for secrecy, Zechariah Chafee, Jr., has pointed out:

No doubt there are many matters which ought not to be disclosed for a time, but the officials should not have a free hand to determine what those matters are or to lock them up forever. It may be human nature for them to want their mere say-so to be decisive on the need for secrecy, but the possession of such a power would allow them to hoist public safety as an umbrella to cover their own mistakes.[10]

In this area, no course is free from risk. If we put freedom in jeopardy, to achieve security, we may wind up by losing both our freedom and our security; if we put our security in too much jeopardy, we may end with the same disaster. This is the dilemma of our age. It is never more serious to our safety than when those responsible for security do not even acknowledge that there is a dilemma.

What can be done to reconcile our traditional freedoms with the requirements of security?

### Committee for Economic Development

The Research and Policy Committee of the Committee for Economic Development has recommended that one full-time civilian member of the National Security Council be made responsible for 'a more effective flow to the public of information relating to national security.' Such an official, they suggested, should 'study all security regulations and recommend to the President changes designed to provide all possible access to information without sacrifice of basic security.'

In its report the Committee said:

It will be necessary to keep security regulations under continual study to make sure that the curtain of secrecy is not drawn tighter than necessary. Some information must be withheld. But we believe that the regulations could be so drawn as to provide the citizen with much more information than he now receives.

More important than the letter of a regulation is the spirit in which it is administered. At present there is a one-sided emphasis upon the importance of secrecy in the indoctrination of officers both military and non-military. A government official is rarely commended for disclosure. He may, however, be reprimanded or otherwise disciplined for 'under-classification,' that is, for failure to make material confidential or secret. A better balance between secrecy and disclosure will give the citizen a sounder basis for exercising responsibility without impairing the administration of security. Among the administrative practises to which attention needs to be paid is the custom of leaving classification in the hands of subordinates, especially clerks or secretaries. The resulting resistance to disclosure can be overcome only if there is positive pressure to release information.[11]

Such an official, functioning effectively, no doubt could remedy an essential weakness in the administration of Executive Order 10-501 — its failure to provide for any system of continuous and concurrent review of classifying activities by agencies other than those doing the classifying.

This official also could become a sort of 'appeals court' to which persons in the government could go to get improper and overzealous classifications changed and one to which private persons could appeal for the release of improperly classified information, if they could discover any. The President's secretary for the press was entrusted with such duties in the Truman administration and the President's General Counsel was given this task in the Eisenhower administration. Both offices, unfortunately, had a great many other duties that did not leave them much time for these tasks.

Were such an official established in the National Security Council, he would have difficulties similar to those which plagued the various Consumers Councils of the New Deal's National Recovery Administration and Agricultural Adjustment Administration. These officials, with the duty of holding prices down for consumers, found themselves in organizations devoted to getting prices up. A 'disclosure' official in the National Security Council would be surrounded by persons primarily interested in withholding information.

John P. Roche suggested that such an official be appointed in the Executive Office of the President, with the task of overseeing all the executive agencies. He declared:

Line agencies [the State Department, Defense Department, AEC, etc.] uniformly tend to exaggerate the importance and secrecy of their activities and to apply higher security standards than an informed outsider would consider justified by the facts. The appointment of such an administrator, who would have the authority to review and revise the decisions below, would provide a central focus and eliminate the confusion and anarchy that now exist. In addition, the line agencies, knowing their decisions to be subject to review, would exercise considerably more care and discrimination than now is the case, and, on the opposite side of the fence, journalistic playing off of one agency against another would be discouraged.[12]

Roche also suggested that this administrator prepare for the press a Code of Security Practices:

This document would be similar in function to the Press Code which Byron Price, Director of the Office of Censorship, prepared in January 1942, for the war-time guidance of the nation's editors. While purely advisory, this code would give the journalist a good idea of what information should be handled with circumspection. In cases of doubt, editors could consult with the administrator before publishing, but the final decision on publication would rest with the newspapers.[13]

An administrator, directly under the President, with these express duties, probably would be more satisfactory than an official handling these problems in addition to other duties, and might be more practical than an official in the National Security Council dominated by a climate of secrecy. A press code, such as that used in the Office of Censorship in World War II, might be preferable to a limitless, guideless avoidance of any information that might be useful to a potential enemy. So much of the success of World War II censorship depended on the personality of Byron Price, its administrator, that support for this system may be more a personal tribute to him than an endorsement of the principle. An administrator of different inclination and philosophy might make such a code an instrument of news suppression. The same sort of administrator who failed to get the White House support that Byron Price invariably received might be far less effectual.

Many such plans might work in a climate favorable to the right of citizens to know. On the other hand, in a climate more favorable to the right to know it might not be necessary to adopt such plans at all. Under any plan or system it will require some administrative ingenuity, operating under a favorable philosophy, to balance the requirements of the nation's safety and the people's information.

# 5

---

## The Right To Know About
## Private Transactions

*Never do anything in secret or anything that you would
wish to hide. For the desire to hide anything means that
you are afraid, and fear is a bad thing and unworthy of
you . . . Privacy, of course, we may have and should
have, but that is a very different thing from secrecy.*
— JAWAHARLAL NEHRU.*

How much do people have a right to know about the transactions of private persons, as distinguished from those of government?

This is a question that cannot be answered with an absolute
'nothing,' or an absolute 'everything.'

Here, as in the case of the information given or withheld
at the discretion of the executive departments of government,
we have long lived with a contradiction.

The right of privacy, as Dr. Harold Cross has pointed out,[1]
was not mentioned by Blackstone, Kent, Hobbes, Rousseau,
or any of the great common law commentators or political

* Jawaharlal Nehru, *Glimpses of World History*, The John Day
Company, 1948, p. 2.

writers. At the turn of the century, American law on the subject began to change. As the result of public reaction against
publications in the press regarded as an invasion of privacy,
the right of privacy has had recognition of varying sorts in
New York, Georgia, Alabama, Alaska, Arizona, California,
Colorado, Florida, Illinois, Indiana, Kansas, Kentucky, Loui-
siana, Michigan, Missouri, New Jersey, North Carolina, Oklahoma, Oregon, Pennsylvania, South Carolina, Utah, Virginia,
and the District of Columbia.[2]

How is it to be decided whether the public's right to know
or the individual's right to privacy is to govern? A New York
court has declared that each case must be decided by 'weighing
the conflicting policies' of 'the public interest in free dissemination of information against the interest in the preservation of
the inviolate personality.' [3]

The law seems to say that the people have the right to know
and that private persons have the right to keep them from
knowing. Which is to be paramount seems to vary, case by
case.

Whatever the law on the matter, as a practical and logical
thing, citizens would seem to have a right to know a great deal
about many business enterprises of a private character. Their
right will be the more indisputable when exercised in reference
to firms that have a public utility role. It certainly remains
substantial where the relation of the private business is even
less direct and may be no more than that of a large supplier
of consumer requirements or a large employer of labor.

The right of privacy, in the sense that that right belongs
to an individual private citizen, certainly cannot be asserted
for some of our great corporations. Woodrow Wilson tried
to point up the legitimate public interest in these concerns.
He said:

A modern joint stock corporation cannot in any proper sense be
said to base its rights and powers upon the principles of private
property. Its powers are wholly derived from legislation. It possesses them for the convenience of business at the sufferance of the

public. Its stock is widely owned, passes from hand to hand, brings multitudes of men into its shifting partnerships, and connects it with the interests and the investments of whole communities. It is a segment of the public; bears no analogy to a partnership or to the processes by which private property is safeguarded and managed, and should not be suffered to afford any covert whatever to those who are managing it. Its management is of public and general concern, is in a very proper sense everybody's business. The business of many of those corporations which we call public-service corporations, and which are indispensable to our daily lives and serve us with transportation and light and water and power, — their business, for instance, is clearly public business; and therefore, we can and must penetrate their affairs by the light of examination and discussion.[4]

The degree to which the statutes sanction this 'examination' of corporate affairs it is not our purpose to examine. Suffice it to say that the principle of disclosure has been given acknowledgment in such enactments as the Securities Exchange Act and in laws that govern public utility companies of many kinds. Few dispute the right of citizens to have access, as investors, to the facts about corporations whose stocks are listed. Few quarrel with the right of the public to know the facts about the operation of utilities, the rates of which must be governed by their operating costs.

Beyond this field, in the area of enterprises, the relation of which is only that of a supplier and an employer, the merits of the case are not so clear and the right to know not so universally acknowledged. Does the public have a right to know everything about the operation of an enterprise simply because it employs other citizens? And if it does, how many citizens is it to be permitted to employ before it loses utterly all right to the privacy of its payroll records, earning reports, profit and loss statements, and production secrets? Does the public have a right to know everything about the operation of an enterprise related to the public solely by its position as a supplier of goods?

These questions certainly lie in an area, legally, where there are many doubts and disputes. Whether the members of a union have or do not have the right to examine the pay records of an employer is a matter now before the courts. Exactly what the public has a right to know about private business is in a state of definition, in detail, and probably will be for a long time to come.

Legal issues aside, however, there are few private businesses that touch the general public's welfare at any point who any longer would subscribe to the abrupt dictum: 'The public be damned!'

Private companies in the United States, in most cases, acknowledge that the people have a right to know a great deal about their operations. Those who manage them live under many of the same compulsions that make it wise for government to be candid, frank, and communicative. Institutions of private as well as of public character cannot retain the confidence of the community in an atmosphere of secrecy. Whatever their strictly legal right to withhold the reasons for firing a manager, promoting a superintendent or moving a plant, changing a shift, tearing down a building or adding a new product, the practical reasons for disclosure outweigh all the legal rights of secrecy.

There may be a strong inclination to maintain silence, to cover up or to conceal, but private enterprise has discovered long since that, in the long run, the price of secrecy is too high to make it a practical policy. The voter who has the power to withhold his ballot for a government official is a customer who has the power to withhold his patronage from a private agency. The habit of indulging democracy is too contagious to be confined to only part of the community's life. People think they have a great deal of right to know about the private institutions that determine their economic environment. The acknowledgment of that right permits the force of public opinion to make itself felt in the making of the policies of private organizations. This phenomenon gives to wholly private efforts an aspect of democracy that is described nowhere in the law and that is not commonly identified in the public mind with the American private enterprise system. If there is any area of American life in which the trend is still toward, and not away from, acknowledgment of the right to know, it is in the area of private business.

There are also a great many nonprofit organizations of essentially private character about which citizens assert a right to know.

Welfare and pension funds, in a sense, are private institutions about which citizens generally may have no strict legal right to know. Yet, more and more people of experience are coming to believe that public scrutiny of such institutions can provide for them the same sort of protection against fraud, corruption, irregularity, and mismanagement that it provides for strictly public institutions.

The Subcommittee on Welfare and Pension Funds of the Senate Committee on Labor and Public Welfare, in its report submitted in January 1955, touched upon the usefulness of such public access to these agencies. It said:

> The subcommittee is convinced that complete disclosure provides the most effective single deterrent to malpractice, mismanagement, and waste. Therefore, consideration should be given to the feasibility of requiring all private employee welfare and pension plans and funds to register and to file annual reports with a Federal agency, on a form to be prescribed by such agency, the information to be made available to all interested parties.[5]

Strictly speaking, many such organizations may owe an accounting only to their members. In a larger sense, however, their adequate and honest management is of more concern than to members and administrators alone. As these funds fail or succeed to carry the social burdens of unemployment or illness or retirement, the burden upon public agencies will be lightened or increased. The whole community has an interest in pension fund management, therefore, beyond its interest in preventing fraud and illegal action generally.

Frequently groups of citizens seek to impose secrecy upon

gatherings of private individuals called to discuss public measures. To what extent do these groups have a right to withhold from the public information of their proceedings? This
is a particularly interesting question when the gatherings
involved are without any legal status or are of undoubted private character.

The public's right to know seems on solid ground where the
organization involved is a quasi-public agency, even though
it has only an informal or social connection with public institutions. A parent-teacher association, for example, is a
private association of citizens and parents and teachers. It has,
however, a certain public status. When it debates the policy
of a school district it becomes, in fact, a part of the government
apparatus of the district, even though the relationship is not
set forth in the law and the actions taken have no formal legal
effect. When such groups meet to plan community actions
that will result in the expenditure of public funds, the raising
of public taxes, or the alteration of public policy, they move
into an area in which the people have a right to know. Citizens
not present have a right to know how and why recommendations were reached.

Parent-teacher groups in Alexandria, Virginia, in 1954, held
secret discussions on the problems of integration in the
schools. Perhaps they had a legal right to do so. It would be
hard to discover any enforceable right to make them meet in
public. Yet, the whole concept of secrecy in the debate of
public questions is at war with democratic theory. It is not
only at war with democratic theory but it is also at war with
good sense in community relations. Secrecy in public gatherings is an invitation to irresponsible utterance. The man who
speaks with the knowledge that the whole community is privy
to his utterance will talk more temperately and judiciously and
accurately if he knows he speaks in the presence of the whole
community. It is not possible, in any case, to hold a really
secret meeting of large numbers of citizens. Those who
manage such gatherings do not have a choice between secrecy

and publicity. They have a choice between an accurate report of a meeting of responsible people and an inaccurate report of a meeting so conducted as to encourage irresponsibility.

When private organizations take important policy steps that are of great public importance and interest, does the public have a right to know about it?

A church in Danville, Virginia, in 1954, decided to abandon its historic policy of segregated worship and conduct its services on an integrated basis. Did the public have a right to know about it? Members of the congregation thought not and attempted to prevent photographic evidence of the mixed services from being made. How are the rights of such groups to the privacy of religious worship and the rights of the public to know to be reconciled? In the past few years religious groups throughout the country, in the conduct of their churches and of their schools, have made great changes in racial policy. Did they have a right to do it in secret or did the public have a right to know? Most of them seemed to think the public had a right to know about such important decisions of private bodies, even though publication in many cases made their task more difficult.

How far has a strictly private organization the right to keep a part of a public meeting on the record and a part of it off the record?

In December 1954, when Norman Cousins, editor of the *Saturday Review*, was speaking to a Toledo audience, he sought to put part of his remarks off the record. Paul Block, Jr., publisher of the *Toledo Blade*, rose and walked out of the meeting in protest. Is it in accord with public policy to allow such off-the-record statements?

The legal aspects of the matter have not been much explored. The private organization no doubt has a strictly legal right to hold a closed meeting. Probably it has a right to ask that part of the meeting be regarded as closed or secret. At the same time, it certainly has no enforceable legal right to prevent those present from reporting the proceedings. Legal issues apart, should private clubs and associations hold secret meetings or have off-the-record sessions?

It is possible to imagine circumstances in which a speaker might wish to disclose to a limited group that which he would not wish to divulge to the whole world. Yet, it is a fair question to ask whether any possible advantages of convenience gained by this device are not outweighed by the risks involved. What are some of the risks?

There are certain very real risks involved if a speaker assumes privacy in order to make disclosures that involve a breach of security or confidentiality. Ordinarily it is not possible to assure that any well-attended meeting really is off the record. It will be reported in some fashion. Those who are naive enough to believe this not the case speak under a false impression.

There are also very serious dangers involved if the cloak of 'off-the-record' is used to cover personal attacks upon individuals. The speakers, by acquiring an imagined immunity to prosecution for scandalous utterance, are encouraged to recklessness. The victims of their reckless accusations, in the absence of any accurate reports, are rendered unable either to meet the charges or to take legal action, with the same facility. The off-the-record meeting may be made a blind from which unscrupulous persons may launch serious reflections upon the conduct of others.

In 1946, a reserve Army officer who had served with the Fifth Army in Italy, in a succession of off-the-record luncheon and dinner meetings, made scandalous allegations about the impiety of Fifth Army officers whom he accused of wanton bombardment of the great monastery at Monte Cassino. None of the officials thus attacked was even aware of these serious reflections on his character and upon the character of the armed forces. Finally, a luncheon guest who disregarded the injunction to secrecy divulged the nature of the attack. The reaction of the accused officers was swift and effective. The attacks upon them ceased.

Secret meetings and gatherings and off-the-record speeches and statements always stand in the danger of such abuses. The best defense against careless utterance and loose accusation lies in publicity. As it improves the quality of the evidence offered in an open court, so it improves the quality of the 'evidence' submitted to a public gathering.

Off-the-record news conferences, in which public men 'brief' a small group of newspapermen, have come into more and more frequent use in American public life. They can be useful to provide background and understanding, either to enlarge reporters' grasp of public issues or to pass on to readers information that could not properly be released with attribution. The 'testimony' that is offered in such sessions, however credible the witness, is under the handicap of all star chamber proceedings and ought to be heard with the reservation that no witness is as reliable in closed testimony as he might be in public testimony. The public man, at such sessions, is under the temptation to contradict in confidence that which he felt compelled to state in public. He may contradict secretly and quite honestly that which he has been forced to subscribe to publicly and falsely, by the policy of his superiors, by the necessities of policy, or the requirements of diplomacy. By affording a convenient opportunity for such contradiction an inducement to hypocrisy is afforded the devious. As a means of giving the press and radio the background against which subsequent developments can be judged, such meetings may be useful. As a substitute for formal, open, and public conferences, off-the-record meetings certainly are unacceptable. The people have a right to know what public men say to groups of citizens — whatever their occupation. To this extent, such confidential exchanges probably come close to violating that right and to appropriating for a small group knowledge to which other citizens have equal right.

What of the more purely private affairs of citizens? How much are the people as a whole entitled to know about them?

It is not uncommon to encounter citizens who think that nothing they may do with their own property is 'anyone else's business.' Yet, society has some concern even here. In the language of Walter Lippmann:

. . . private property can never be regarded as giving to any man an absolute title to exercise 'the sole and despotic dominion' over the land and the resources of nature. The ultimate title does not lie in the owner. The title is in 'mankind,' in The People as a corporate community.[6]

So what a man does even with his own property is of public concern, and if what he does violates the interest of society, the people assuredly have a right to know about it. The right of privacy cannot be claimed to shield the man who would destroy land or buildings, in which the whole community has an interest. Nor can it be used to protect those who would wantonly destroy some priceless work of art or some relic of history that, wherever private title lies, is essentially the inheritance of all mankind.

Nor are all the strictly nonpublic relations of a citizen with other citizens wholly private. The public's right to know is, of course, clear where laws are violated. It may even be debatable where only convention is violated. The theoretical legal right of the individual to do as he chooses, without the knowledge of his fellows, diminishes as the consequences of what he chooses become of greater concern to his contemporaries.

In the words of John Donne, 'No man is an *Iland*, intire of it selfe . . .' What happens to any human being is of concern to all others. At its worst, the curiosity of people to know of the affairs of others may be mean, prying, offensive, and obscene. At its best, this all-pervading curiosity, so deeply implanted in man, is an acknowledgment of the oneness of mankind of which Donne wrote. The appetite for privacy, and secrecy, so far as it concerns the desire to be sheltered from the public gaze, in the sanctity of the home, in the pursuit of domestic ends wholly unrelated to all other men, may be a natural one. But there are few acts that men perform that are utterly beyond the concern of any citizen's fellow men. And the more crowded the world becomes, the fewer they are. Public curiosity is not to be indulged at the expense of all privacy; but it may be said of a steadily diminishing number of things: 'That's my business!'

The more that a man is a public man the fewer these things are, and the more he is a strictly private man the more they are; but public or private, people have a right to know about a great many strictly private acts which the complexity of our society now invests with public interest.

It is a nice legal problem to try to decide what acts of the public man are his own concern alone and to try to fix what acts of a private person ought to lie beyond all public scrutiny. What people have a right to know probably will be governed less by law than by the ingenuity with which they assert the right, for a long time to come. What privacy the individual has a right to enforce against the curiosity of the public likewise probably will depend, for a long time ahead, upon the ingenuity and energy with which the private person asserts the right to conceal his personal affairs.

The balance of these rights is in a constant state of change, and none can say at what point they will come into some kind of equilibrium in which people will be able to know as much as they ought to know without transforming all human existence into life in a goldfish bowl.

# 6

---

## THE RIGHT TO PRINT WITHOUT PRIOR RESTRAINT

*And though all the winds of doctrine were let loose to play upon the earth, so Truth be in the field, we do injuriously by licensing and prohibiting to misdoubt her strength.* — MILTON, *Areopagitica*

FROM 1538 to 1695 the struggle for freedom of the press, in England, was largely a struggle against licensing.

The proclamation of 1538, issued by Henry VIII, put the whole press under a licensing system. All who sought to publish were required to submit their intended works, prior to publication, for official approval and censorship. Religious works were scrutinized by the clergy; political works by the government, at first. For intervals, heresy and treason were almost indistinguishable crimes.

The freedom of the press lay under this burden, in various forms, until the lapse of the last licensing act in 1695.

It is not remarkable that a struggle which cost so many lives and extended over so many years put so great an emphasis upon the importance of licensing as to cause many to believe that the freedom from prior restraint, the escape from censorship, and the emergence from licensing constituted the whole of press freedom.

Hallam's *Constitutional History of England* declares that 'Liberty of the press consists, in a strict sense, merely in an exemption from the superintendence of a licenser.'

Sir William Blackstone declared: 'The liberty of the press is indeed essential to the nature of a free state; but this consists in laying no previous restraints upon publications. . .' [1]

This is by no means all there is to freedom of the press. Zechariah Chafee, Jr., has pointed out that this Blackstonian definition is not an interpretation of the American Constitution, but a statement of English law at the time, and one out of harmony with English law of the last 125 years. He has described the theory of Blackstone as 'inconsistent with eighteenth-century history . . . contrary to modern decisions, thoroughly artificial, and wholly out of accord with a common-sense view of the relations of state and citizen.' [2]

Our First Amendment, Cooley has pointed out, was intended to do much more than merely secure the press against licensing.

The evils to be prevented were not the censorship of the press merely, but any action of the government by means of which it might prevent such free and general discussion of public matters as seems absolutely essential to prepare the people for an intelligent exercise of their rights as citizens.[3]

In the catalog of those rights essential to a free press, none probably is less vulnerable to frontal attack. The most indifferent citizens would hardly be likely to view lightly legislation or executive order imposing a universal censorship or setting up a system of press licensing.

If this one of our press freedoms has been made relatively secure by the long struggle through which it was established, by its conspicuous place in the history of our institutions, by the ease with which formal licensing and censorship can be identified, it still is by no means utterly safe.

It is not safe because there are means of requiring prior

restraint in less obvious ways than those employed from Henry VIII to Queen Elizabeth. There are means of imposing censorship not so conspicuous as licensing acts.

To say that the freedom from prior restraint is not all there is to freedom of the press is not to say that it is unimportant to freedom of the press. It is vitally and indispensably important. We must be constantly on the alert to detect impairment of this freedom, however subtle.

Americans have been justifiably disquieted by experiments in this direction. The approach to press licensing under the National Industrial Recovery Act of the first administration of Franklin Roosevelt deserved the resistance that was encountered. Concern has been created by the enactment of Public Law 557, which became effective on 29 July 1954, and under which organizations required to register under the Internal Security Act of 1950 must register all equipment in their possession, custody, or control for printing or publishing any printed matter.

This law is a good illustration of the difficulty of deciding at precisely what point a fundamental freedom is menaced. Few citizens are likely to be alarmed by restraints laid upon political groups with which the overwhelming majority is so completely out of sympathy. The risk, of course, is that once having allowed registration of the presses in the hands of certain unpopular groups, what is to prevent Congress from requiring registration of the presses of additional groups?

It is not easy, either, to decide at what point mere registration becomes equal to licensing. The Swedish constitution, which has so many excellent provisions on press freedom, requires the registration of a printing establishment in the county in which it is located, at least two weeks prior to the first print issued.[4]

In the context of the liberal Swedish constitution, it may be doubted that this simple act of registration is a serious menace to freedom of the press.

However, in other climates and under constitutions not

otherwise so clear, it might well be fatal to press freedom. Operation of a secret press, to which so many peoples in so many lands have at various times been indebted for the preservation of their liberties, would be rendered infinitely more precarious under such a statute. In a country, and under a government, hostile to all press criticism, the very act of registration would constitute a disclosure fatal to freedom of the press.

The risks involved presently in Public Law 557 may not appear alarming. Yet, it could be extended by statute, or even by construction of the law requiring registration of subversive groups, so as to embrace not only Communist and like subversive organization presses, but the presses of others desiring to express dissent of a wholly different sort.

Is the danger which this law attempts to reach worth the risks that it involves? In measuring both the danger and the risks, we need to consider the future as well as the present. The question is not only: What is the risk today? We must ask: What will be the risk at some future date when this law is at hand for a government determined to crush all press opposition?

In spite of our relative security against direct licensing, it is evident that something very close to licensing has been enacted, with very little public notice. If it is not licensing, it is the closest thing to it that has been seen since the adoption of the Constitution. Whether or not it is consistent with the First Amendment is for the United States Supreme Court to say.

In spite of the First Amendment's ban on prior restraint of the press, censorship of the press has been frequent in American history.

In wartime the government has imposed censorship in combat theaters, and in World War I and World War II it operated censorship in the zone of the interior. These lapses from the full enforcement of the First Amendment have been countenanced under the liberal construction of the emergency powers required to save the country — powers of self-preservation that seem inherent in sovereignty.

Operation under the Atomic Energy Act also has involved a kind of prior restraint and advance censorship. This has grown out of the fact that the law precludes the publication of information on nuclear science not cleared for publication by the Atomic Energy Commission. In order to find out what has been cleared, newspapers have frequently found it advisable to submit to the Atomic Energy Commission material intended for publication, before printing it. The Act reversed the conventional military theory under which the press was permitted to publish anything not proscribed, and applied the rule that nothing was to be published unless cleared. Here again there had to be a weighing of risks and dangers. No doubt national opinion once supported, and it may still support, this policy, preferring the dangers of censorship to the risks of compromising atomic secrets. The dangers are minimized here by the closely specified area to which censorship is confined; but it must be acknowledged that Congress has passed and the country has acquiesced in a plain exception to the First Amendment's ban on prior restraint.

This ban may be interfering with the country's rapid utilization of atomic energy for peaceful uses. It has piled up in the classified envelopes of AEC some eighty million documents already, and experts engaged in declassification find it difficult to keep up with the flood of material. Information on the construction of power reactors has been released and declassified so that private industry is able to proceed on contracts for their construction. What industry cannot know, and what it has not been told, however, is whether or not the AEC retains under classification information on more efficient and effective reactors. Industry knows how to build one type of reactor. Are there other, cheaper, and better types? And may information about them be released and declassified after plants have been built according to plans presently declassified?

This ignorance and doubt produces a state of insecurity for

the few large firms capable of financing such construction. In such uncertainty, it is not easy to interest responsible company directors in ventures running into costs of millions of dollars.

More and more personnel are being put to work by AEC on the task of declassification.

As long as the present law is in effect, however, there always will be some brake on peacetime uses of atomic energy. New information automatically falls under classification, wherever it is originated. The process of its accumulation will be swifter each year and it will be progressively more difficult for declassifying operations to keep up with it. This will impose a lag on private utilization of atomic information. It is difficult to estimate the seriousness of this lag. When we find out how serious it is, we may be far behind countries that have handled the matter differently. Curiously enough, we may lag behind both the countries with less secrecy and greater private access and behind those (such as Soviet Russia) with greater secrecy and no private access whatever. In the case of the latter, of course, the fullest construction does not have to await private investors' confidence or their full information.

The real risks in the censorship imposed by the military authorities in combat areas and on military installations and that enforced by the Atomic Energy Commission lie in the temptation to push the censorship beyond allowable boundaries. It is not always easy for untrained personnel to distinguish between material that endangers security and that which only threatens to embarrass.

Recently, an officer in the Pentagon who asked to see photographs of the restaurant operation in that building, before their publication, urged the omission of photographs that showed the wall menu, including prices. Not the slightest element of security was involved, but it is not always easy to distinguish between policy and security. Once the right to censor for security reasons has been acknowledged, it is no longer as easy to maintain the same solid resistance to censorship of any kind.

The Constitution may protect against the exercise of prior restraint on publication by congressional enactment, but what about prior restraint employed by executive agencies with the consent of the press? Many publications feared this might be involved in the Office of Strategic Information set up in the Commerce Department in 1954 for the purpose of diminishing the flow of technical information that might be of use to an enemy. A government bureau, without a single statute to support it, in a time of fear and panic, no doubt could get nearly all publications to submit to restraints on publication of prescribed data. A press that would tamely submit to censorship and prior restraint would not deserve many tears. However, the constitutional immunity to prior restraint was not devised for the benefit of newspapers but for the information of the people. Such a consent to prior restraint would imperil their access to information as much as a legally enforceable consorship.

The authors of the Bill of Rights were clearly trying to protect citizens against a system under which the information permitted to them might fall under the control of government. It is doubtful if they would find censorship enforced by a conspiracy of office holders and editors any less offensive than one enforced by Congress.

This is an aspect of freedom that ought to be kept in mind by newspaper editors and reporters when they are brought into a degree of collaboration with officials. There is a very fine line indeed separating this kind of co-operation from prior restraint under law.

This sort of 'co-operation' can be made to sound very palatable and reasonable. Arias Delgado of the Spanish Ministry of Information has explained that in Spain, 'previous consultation' is only a 'preventive function of harmonious co-operation and tutelage for the common good.'[5]

Conscientious publications, anxious to avoid breeches of

security, in recent years have developed a practice of 'clearing' matter of questionable safety with government agencies involved. This is an inescapable necessity so far as atomic matter is concerned. It may be advisable where editors are in doubt about other security material. It is easy to move from here, however, into clearance for policy considerations. Government officials consulted on security matters find it difficult to restrain an impulse to suggest changes that will put an agency in a better public light, a temptation to put forward alterations that will soften an adverse opinion or put an official in a more favorable posture. This is fine for relations between government and press but it may deprive the public of the sort of critical appraisal that the authors of the Bill of Rights were trying to preserve.

When Jefferson said that no government ought to be without a critic and that none would be as long as the press was free, he had in mind a press that did not have to 'clear' its views on government with the very departments and agencies being criticized.

The sudden emergence of radio broadcasting as a means of communication presented the government with problems the solution of which was not to be found in past experience with the press. The flat and explicit ban of the Constitution on licensing and prior censorship posed no insoluble practical problems. The country never reached the point of saturation in the number of presses at which their operation interfered with each other. Many European critics of the American press thought that newspapers were so numerous, in the nineteenth century, as to lower the quality of all of them. No one ever suggested that government reduce the number by licensing. The number of presses was unlimited and competition could be left to diminish the ranks of the newspapers.

Radio had differences instantly apparent. The number of channels was limited. They had to be allocated. Once allocated, it was necessary that the stations be required to stay on their authorized channels and utilize authorized power.

The alternative was a chaos of conflicting signals in which none of the stations could have been heard. Obviously no private power was equal to the task of allocation or enforcement. Government assumption of the obligation was inevitable. This meant, inescapably, government licensing of a media differing from the press only in the mechanical device employed to disseminate information. Government was thus propelled into a sort of licensing which every constitutional authority until the advent of radio would have described as unconstitutional.

The Communications Act of 1934 authorized the Federal Communications Commission to make rules and regulations required by public convenience, interest, or necessity 'not inconsistent with law.'

The programs of stations, the information and entertainment that they dispensed, quickly and perhaps inevitably became an element in the decisions of public necessity. And as soon as the programs of the stations came under the purview of the Commission, and entered into judgments involving the issuance and extension of licenses, government found itself knee-deep in an enterprise that surely would have been abhorrent to every one of the founding fathers.

The Mayflower opinion of 1941 illuminated the dangers involved. The Commission reproached Station WAAB for broadcasting editorials urging the election of various candidates for political office. It stated flatly that 'a truly free radio cannot be used to advocate the causes of the licensee. It cannot be used to support the candidates of his friends. It cannot be used to support the principles he happens to regard most favorably. . . These requirements are inherent in the conception of public interest set up by the Communications Act as the criterion of regulation.'

The radio station committed itself not to editorialize in the future and on this promise its license was renewed. The Commission thereby bluntly exercised governmental power to restrain future utterance or 'publication' in the precise manner the First Amendment was intended to restrain.

The principles which governed the Communications Commission in this proceeding and those which governed the United States Supreme Court in Near *v.* Minnesota on 1 June 1931 are simply irreconcilable. They were separated in point of time by only a decade; they are a world apart in philosophy.

A Minnesota statute provided for the abatement, as a public nuisance, of a 'malicious, scandalous, and defamatory' newspaper, magazine, or other periodical, and also of obscene periodicals. Courts were empowered to issue injunctions stopping the convicted newspapers entirely. The law was invoked against the *Saturday Press*, charged by the county attorney with being largely devoted to 'malicious, scandalous, and defamatory articles.' The paper was closed by the courts. Near, the manager, lost in an appeal to the state supreme court. The case was then carried to the United States Supreme Court.

The case of the *Saturday Press*, of course, was a much worse case than that of the Mayflower Broadcasting Company. No one had charged the Mayflower Broadcasting Company with being 'malicious, scandalous, and defamatory.' It was only accused of being 'editorial' or 'partisan.'

The United States Supreme Court found the Minnesota gag law repugnant to the First Amendment. An opinion, written by the Chief Justice, bluntly described it as 'the essence of censorship.' The Court pointed out that 'the general conception of liberty of the press, historically considered and taken up by the Federal Constitution, has meant principally although not exclusively, immunity from previous restraints or censorship. The conception of the liberty of the press in this country had broadened with the exigencies of the colonial period and with the efforts to secure freedom from oppressive administration. That liberty was especially cherished for the immunity it afforded from previous restraint of the publication of censure of public officers and charges of official misconduct.'

The Court concluded:

The fact that for approximately one hundred and fifty years there has been almost an entire absence of attempts to impose previous restraints upon publications relating to the malfeasance of public officers is significant of the deep-seated conviction that such restraints would violate constitutional right. Public officers whose character and conduct remain open to debate and free discussion in the press find their remedies for false accusations in actions under libel laws providing for redress and punishment, and not in proceedings to restrain the publication of newspapers and periodicals.[6]

Of this decision and opinion Zechariah Chafee wrote:

Its strong hostility to previous restraints against the expression of ideas may conceivably be applied to quite different forms of censorship, affecting other media of communication besides the press. Newspapers, books, pamphlets, and large meetings were for many centuries the only means of public discussion, so that the need for their protection has been generally realized. On the other hand, when additional methods for spreading facts and ideas were introduced or greatly improved by modern inventions, writers and judges had not got into the habit of being solicitous about guarding their freedom. And so we have tolerated censorship of the mails, the importation of foreign books, the stage, the motion picture, and the radio. In an age when the film and broadcasting station have become rivals of the newspaper for the transmission of news, the new judicial attitude evidenced in Near v. Minnesota may have important consequences.[7]

Up to the present time, there has been no real opportunity for the United States Supreme Court to apply to radio and television the plain principles of Near v. Minnesota. Those who remain in business at the precarious pleasure of the licenser have not dared push a challenge to the highest court, apparently. So we have the curious paradox of a Supreme Court opinion stating that government may not stop a newspaper, even if it is or has been 'defamatory,' while an agency of government threatens to stop a radio station for statements merely 'editorial' and not even alleged to be defamatory.

It was evident, from the beginning, that the very exercise of licensing power ran the risk of this kind of censorship. The most apprehensive thought that such censorship, although never publicly professed or openly asserted, would so influence the licensing decisions of the Commission. Even the most fearful did not anticipate in 1934 that the Commission by 1941 would be openly asserting not only the right to reproach a licensee for past utterance but the authority to govern his future utterance.

Is such authority inseparable from licensing? So the advocates of a free press, as it is conceived in our Constitution, have thought for 150 years. It will be a real test of political ingenuity to discover some system by which order can be maintained on the air without the risk of censorship.

Such flagrancies as the Mayflower case probably do not represent the commonest danger. The criticism that it provoked, and the reaction later to the Federal Communication Commission's blue book, suggest that formal assertion of authority over programs may be more infrequent in the future than in the past. Yet, the shadow of the Commission's authority lies over all radio and television stations, inhibiting their comment on political issues to whatever degree the individual station management may fear that what is uttered over the station may jeopardize the renewal of his license.

Perhaps this fear is a minimal factor in the decisions of stations in the hands of rich and powerful individuals or corporations. The First Amendment was devised to protect, not only the liberty of the rich and the powerful, but that of the lowliest citizen. To make the radio really free, some means must be found by which the FCC can be divested of the power to withhold licenses for engaging in precisely the sort of political comment and criticism that the framers of the First Amendment wished to preserve.

The controversy over pay television has served to emphasize how inconsistent and improper is the government's relation to broadcasting. Only time will prove whether it is or is not feasible to charge users for television programs. Government, however, ought to be no more involved in this decision than it has been involved in the past in the decision of the press on the same question. Newspapers and periodicals have come to their several, differing choices on whether to put their reliance upon the payments of the subscribers or those of the advertisers. Government intervention in the decision would have been spurned by the press, denounced by the people, and refused by the courts. Whether *Reader's Digest* chooses to get all or part of its revenue from readers, or all or part of it from advertisers, is a decision for *Reader's Digest*. Whether television is to be supported by advertising or admissions ought to be a decision for television. If government stood apart from the issue, competition would decide it sooner or later and probably in somewhat the same fashion that competition has made a like decision in the publications field.

The impropriety of life-or-death control by government of a press intended to be the critic and censor of that same government is so obvious that the point did not have to be argued in our courts for 125 years. The impropriety of the same sort of control over radio and television, which ought to be the same sort of censor and critic of government, is equally obvious. Plain as it is, that control seems to continue without much challenge, either from the broadcasters or from the public.

Few situations better illustrate the difficulty of making any freedom forever secure against encroachment, by constitutional or legislative devices.

The first Congress of the United States must have felt, when it completed the First Amendment, that it had made freedom of the press and freedom of speech as secure against future encroachment as human devices and institutions could make them. It would be difficult to devise plainer language than 'Congress shall make no law . . .' From that day until this there has been no assertion, by Congress or by the courts, to deny that 'censorship and prior restraint' are comprehended within the objects of that prohibition.

Still, such are the differences of opinion on what constitutes censorship and on what constitutes prior restraint that executive agencies, under the sanction of Congress, have trespassed even here.

And of all these trespasses, the Communications Act of 1934 most fully vindicates the judgment of Alexander Hamilton, who wrote in *The Federalist:*

What signifies a declaration, that 'the liberty of the press shall be inviolably preserved?' What is the liberty of the press? Who can give it any definition which would not leave the utmost latitude for evasion? I hold it to be impracticable; and from this I infer, that its security, whatever fine declarations may be inserted in any constitution respecting it, must altogether depend on public opinion, and on the general spirit of the people and of the government.[8]

In the light of our history, few would be willing to abandon the practical protection of freedom of the press that has been conferred upon the American people by the First Amendment. At the same time, it is possible to wish for a public opinion, a 'general spirit of the people and of the government,' more alert to and alarmed by the stealthy erosions of long-established rights.

# 7

---

## REPRISAL FOR PUBLICATION

*But while we concede that liberty of speech and of the press does not imply complete exemption from responsibility for everything a citizen may say or publish, and complete immunity to ruin the reputation or business of others so far as falsehood and detraction may be able to accomplish that end, it is nevertheless believed that the mere exemption from previous restraints cannot be all that is secured by the constitutional provisions, inasmuch as of words to be uttered orally there can be no previous censorship, and the liberty of the press might be rendered a mockery and a delusion, and the phrase itself a byword, if, while every man was at liberty to publish what he pleased, the public authorities might nevertheless punish him for harmless publication.* — THOMAS M. COOLEY ***

THE people will not obtain information if those to whom they look to supply it live under the threat of reprisal for innocent publication, or if the penalties for wrongful publication are such as to make the risks of publishing unbearable.

* Thomas M. Cooley, *Constitutional Limitations*, Little, Brown and Co., Boston, vol. II, p. 885.

Those to whom citizens look for information about their government must be able to get information, they must be free to print it without prior restraint, and they must be safe from this kind of reprisal either by government or by those acting in disregard of or under the sanction of government.

There must exist what Cooley describes as 'complete immunity from legal censure and punishment for the publication, so long as it is not harmful in its character, when tested by such standards as the law affords.'

The freedom with which knowledge and information circulate in a society is greatly influenced by protections afforded against reprisal. It is affected by the legal reprisals available through common law interpretations and the statutes relating to libel, contempt, slander, obscenity, disturbance of the peace, treason by publication, and other offenses by publication that have been known to history. It is also affected by the immunity that the press enjoys against extralegal reprisal by officials acting in disregard of the laws. And it is affected by safety against the reprisal of the mob or of other individuals hostile to published words.

There are few places in the world where those who publish information are as free from the menace of legal reprisal for publications alleged to be wrongful as they are in the United States. The rules of libel, construed from the common law, and the statutes on libel generally are fair and generous. Courts and juries, in the main, have always seemed aware that some latitude must be given if the sources of information are not to be dried up.

Contempt of court, once the terror of the press, and still a menace in many countries, now is so narrowly construed as a result of the United States Supreme Court decisions in the Bridges case and the Pennekamp case that publication must plainly obstruct the processes of justice in order to risk contempt. Privilege, as in the reporting of trials and legislative proceedings, also seems to cover so many public transactions as to leave the press free to report all kinds of public meetings with little risk, so long as the reports are accurate, fair, and impartial. In these areas, the laws continue to exert some restraint on publication, but few would argue that the restraint has at all reached a point where it impairs seriously the willingness to publish or interferes with the public's right to know.

Present day threats, at local and state levels, now arise more frequently in connection with publication that is alleged to be obscene, lewd, and in violation of public morals or good taste. Popular outrage at comic books and girlie magazines has precipitated a wave of ordinances, legislation, and popular reprisal in many parts of the United States.

Punishment for publication that is 'immoral' of course involves the classic risk of all punishment for publication. Someone in official position, ultimately, must decide what is and what is not immoral. There is an astonishing variety of belief on these matters. As soon as power is lodged in government to make these decisions, not only manifestly immoral publication, but all publication is put to some hazard. This hazard is the least ominous when due process is preserved. The good sense of the community has an opportunity to assert itself when there are formal charges, openly heard, tried in a court, and decided by a jury. The sheerest nonsense may govern when the method used to suppress alleged obscenity is the blacklist, blackmail, and intimidation. These risks probably loom larger for the distribution of information than for publication.

The most serious danger of reprisal at the federal level probably arises in connection with the publication of material alleged to involve the military security of the United States. This has been more fully discussed earlier. It ought to be said here, however, that the Atomic Energy Act and the Espionage Act both involve penalties for publication more drastic than ever hitherto employed in peacetime in this country. A prosecuting government might make risks of all publication in this area so great as to seriously diminish public access to information about military affairs.

English history, and the history of colonial America, furnish many examples of governmental reprisal against publications critical of authority.

The right to punish for seditious libel was claimed under English common law for seventy-five years after the end of licensing. Sir James Fitzjames Stephen has pointed out that the seditious libel laws of England, as enforced for decades, were 'wholly inconsistent with any serious public discussion of political affairs.' James Morton Smith, who quotes this opinion in a study, *The Sedition Law*, ventures his own belief that 'As long as it was recognized as the law of the land, any political discussion existed only by sufferance of the government.' [1]

How fatal this form of executive reprisal was to freedom of the press also has been noticed by Macaulay, who observed that 'the liberty of unlicensed printing was of little or no use to the vanquished party; for the temper of the judges was such that no writer whom the government prosecuted for libel had any chance of escaping.'

Macaulay pointed out that 'the dread of punishment therefore did all that a censorship could have done.' [2]

Until the passage of the Fox Libel Act in 1792, the terrors of libel prosecutions were multiplied by rules under which juries were permitted to judge only of the fact of publication, while judges decided on the question of libel itself. The penalties, moreover, were severe. Guilty printers could be transported to the colonies for seven years. William Cobbett was sent to prison for two years and fined a thousand pounds for criticizing flogging in the army in his *Political Register*.[3] The same penalty was imposed on Leigh Hunt and John Hunt for saying in the *Examiner* that the Prince Regent was a 'fat Adonis of fifty.'

John Wilkes dared the libel laws to criticize the King's

Speech to Parliament in No. 45 of the *North Briton*. The Government issued a general warrant for the printers and publishers of the issue, and by a skillful attack on the general warrant, Wilkes at first evaded punishment, but finally was penalized for reprinting the issue.

The principles which the Fox Libel Law put an end to in England were challenged in the colonies earlier. Andrew Hamilton, in his great argument in the Peter Zenger trial in 1734, held the jury to be judge both of the fact of publication and of the question of whether the published matter was libelous. So, long before the end of the colonial period, the common law theories of seditious libel had been challenged in North America.

What was comprehended by 'freedom of the press' when the Bill of Rights was adopted, it is clear, was something a great deal more than freedom from prior restraint. Those who framed it thought they had put an end to other infringements against which a struggle had been made throughout the colonial period.

The first reprisal against an editor, nevertheless, did not wait long after the inauguration of the new government. On 26 June 1798, Benjamin Franklin Bache, grandson of Benjamin Franklin and editor of the Philadelphia *Aurora*, was arrested to answer a Federal common law indictment for seditious libels against the President and the executive branch of the government.[4] In 1795 Bache had printed the complete text of Jay's treaty while the Senate was considering it in secret. He was a defender of the French Revolution and a critic of Washington's domestic and foreign policies. Bache died on 10 September before he could be prosecuted as the first victim of an American action for seditious libel.

Under the Sedition Act, passed in July 1798, thirteen indictments were ground out by Federal enforcement officers, all of them against Republican newspapers critical of the Federalists. James Morton Smith has summarized the cases as follows:

Every man convicted under the Sedition Law was fined and imprisoned for political expressions critical of the administration in power. Indeed, the chief enforcement effort was tied directly to the campaign of 1800. As the contest between Jefferson and Adams approached, the Secretary of State Timothy Pickering made systematic plans for action against the leading Republican newspapers in the United States.[5]

The Sedition Act died with the Adams administration. Public reaction to it was such that state prosecutions for seditious libel grew less and less frequent and finally almost ceased, too.

World War I brought another flurry of prosecutions for seditious utterance. Governmental reprisal for utterance began to revive as early as the 1880's, with a period of labor unrest, but not until 1917 did the threat of government punishment hang over utterance to anything like the extent that it did in the Sedition Act period. Then came the Debs, Berger, and Anita Whitney convictions and other attacks upon individuals for utterances of a seditious tendency.[6]

Utterance came under nothing like the same degree of threat in World War II. Even the postwar period of cold-war tension has not caused as widespread use of governmental authority against utterance only, on the ground of seditious tendency.

Criminal libel cases, few in number, have represented another means of reprisal against antigovernmental utterance.

One of the most sensational efforts to use a criminal libel prosecution to punish utterances critical of the government occurred in 1908. The *Indianapolis News* and the *New York World* attacked the Theodore Roosevelt administration for acts of the United States Government in the purchase of the Canal Zone from Panama, and for purchase of the rights of the French Company to the canal right of way. The *News* published the story first. The *New York World* joined with a lusty attack on Roosevelt and his administration, demanding to know: 'Who Got The Money?' Roosevelt sent a special message to Congress attacking Joseph Pulitzer by name and said the government would prosecute him for criminal libel. Two suits were brought and indictments were returned in the District of Columbia. The newspapers held they could not be forced into a federal court in this manner. The United States Supreme Court upheld them and declared the President without power to institute the suits except in state courts.

There have been some criminal libel actions in the states, from time to time. A recent one was instituted in Maryland against the radio commentator Fulton Lewis for criticism of county officials, in 1953. The prosecution failed.

There are, of course, means other than criminal prosecutions by which a national administration can punish those who attack it by utterance or publication. These means, incidentally, multiply year by year as the powers of the federal government continue to grow. It sometimes is difficult to distinguish between prosecutions undertaken in the normal course of law enforcement and those inspired by a desire for reprisal. Antitrust prosecutions, where construction of the statutes gives wide discretion to authority, frequently are criticized as retaliatory. Actions against the *Kansas City Star* have been criticized on this ground. Whether or not the criticism is justified in this case, the law suit has made it clear that many journalistic operations in a big-newspaper era run the risk of exposing publications to such costly prosecutions. They add another hazard in any period when political opposition is intense.

The vast structure of other federal, state, and local regulatory measures provides another arsenal of weapons with which governmental bodies could harass unfriendly newspapers. The proven and deliberate use of these regulatory measures for the purpose of coercion has been rare in the United States. Many cases of police enforcement of regulations, suddenly tightened up by a department under press criticism to the point of harassment of newspapers, are cited. Few will stand close scrutiny.

The power of government to withdraw favor improperly

or illegally extended has been another means of reprisal. This device has been notoriously employed in some countries where enforcement of import duties against newsprint have been neglected until the newspapers criticized the regime. The accumulated tax evasions then have become a convenient device of reprisal.

Another much-feared form of reprisal is the power of the federal government to withold privileges and licenses and franchises from newspapers. Legislation was introduced in the 84th Congress to prohibit the Federal Communications Commission from discriminating against newspaper ownership of radio and TV stations. A politically minded government certainly could use authority to withhold or deny or cancel TV and radio licenses as a powerful reprisal against newspapers. (Of course, the power to use it against TV and radio stations generally always exists in a licensing system.) If isolated instances of such reprisal have occurred, the fact is that many publications notoriously critical of administrations in power have not been disturbed in their ownership of radio and TV stations. The bills introduced in the 84th Congress reflect an uneasy appreciation of the fact that the power could be abused.

There are many rights and privileges within the gift of the federal administration that are essential to the efficient operation of newspapers and the withholding of which could become an effective means of extralegal reprisal. Admission to the congressional galleries, to the White House, to federal departments — all these could be used in a discriminatory way against offending publications. From time to time, there have been charges of such abuse but the evidence has not supported them.

Until the courts, in 1955, intervened to say that the State Department could not withhold passports without cause and the specification of charges, there was a sharper risk that the right to travel might be withheld arbitrarily from a publication. In July of 1955, the State Department, in spite of the strict letter of passport regulations, permitted Joseph Clark, the United Nations correspondent of the New York *Daily Worker,* to go abroad to cover the Geneva conference. The issuance of the passport, at first tentatively held up, demonstrated the utter unwillingness of the government to take a step that would have even the remotest appearance of punishing by discriminatory treatment a publication held to be odious by the government and by the overwhelming number of citizens. Its action helped further to establish the principle that these rights are not given or withdrawn on the basis of the political beliefs of applicants seeking credentials for foreign reporting.

The possibilities for such reprisals by a politically motivated government, it is apparent, are perfectly enormous. Evidences of a resort to reprisal are, fortunately, not frequent.

### Congressional Reprisal

The framers of the Bill of Rights no doubt thought they had effectively stopped Congress from trespassing upon freedom of the press when they obtained approval of the First Amendment providing that Congress shall pass no law infringing upon it.

Congress has found other means, however, for restraining the press and one of the most effective of these has been legislative reprisal for offensive publication.

Its first such effort was made against William Duane, who on the death of Benjamin Bache had married his widow and succeeded to the job of editor of his paper, the *Aurora.*

Early in 1800, the Federalists began to lay plans by which they hoped to gain the presidential election.

On 23 January 1800, Senator James Ross of Pennsylvania brought in a bill to set up a Grand Committee to settle disputed presidential elections and determine the legality or illegality of electoral votes.[7]

The Committee was to be made up of the Chief Justice, six members of the Senate, and six members of the House. It would meet in secret, examine the qualifications of electors, see if bribery was used, and decide which votes would be counted and which disallowed.

At the same time, the Federalists took steps to save the vote in Pennsylvania. There they had lost the 1799 gubernatorial race. They stood to lose the electoral race unless the Presidential electors were picked by districts rather than by a statewide vote.[8]

These schemes were planned in a secret caucus of seventeen Federalist senators. The proposals were carried by nine votes which bound the whole group.

Three Republican senators gave Duane a copy of the Ross bill, which he printed on 19 February 1800. He denounced its backers as 'the party hostile to the popular interest' and said they wished to 'destroy the popular authority and to engross every power which the people enjoy by the right and constitution in the hands of a few.' He branded the bill as an effort to control the election of 1800. Plainly, the Federalists, by their secret Grand Committee, proposed to find enough trumped-up charges to throw out the Republican votes by which Jefferson might otherwise be elected.

The Federalist senators moved to establish a standing Committee of Privileges to study Duane's offense. The motion carried and the Committee was authorized. It was asked at once to inquire who was the editor of the *Aurora* and how he came to publish a copy of the Ross bill. The Committee reported Duane was the editor and concluded that the publishing of the bill was a high breach of privilege, and that the remarks of Duane were false, defamatory, scandalous, and a libel of a malicious kind. The Senate agreed.

Duane had mistakenly reported the bill passed and he was hotly criticized for this. Duane had protested that Senator Pinckney, a Republican, had not attended the caucus and senators asserted he had.

Senator Uriah Tracy of Connecticut said the Senate had undoubted power to punish interruptions of its proceedings and that Duane's attack was an interruption. He also held the

Senate could not be questioned anywhere at any time by anyone under the rule that it had been given Constitutional immunity.

Senator Charles Pinckney defended Duane. He said there
was nowhere in the Constitution any mention of the right of
either house to order the appearance of a person charged with
printing attacks on the public conduct and to imprison him
at its will.

Pinckney said the founders of the Constitution well knew
to what oppressive use the British Parliament had put the
theory of undefined 'inherent' privileges. He said that they had
accordingly 'specified the few principles necessary to the
undisturbed exercise of legislative duties in a free government.' He said citizens had a right to investigate the conduct
of the legislature. He took note of the charges against Duane
and said:

If a printer was to be seized and dragged before the senate bar and
perhaps imprisoned for mistakenly saying that a law had passed
when it was only in its second reading and that a committeeman
was not notified of a meeting when he was, no reporter would venture to take the debates and the Senate's doors might as well be
closed again.[9]

The Federalists did not answer Pinckney but moved the
adoption of Tracy's motion.

Senator Humphrey Marshall of Kentucky unsuccessfully
attempted to get the Senate to inquire into all breaches of its
privileges by newspapers, whether they were of Federalist or
Republican persuasion.

The Republicans then tried to get the Duane charges referred to the Attorney General to see if a prosecution was
in order. This was also voted down. The committee was in-
structed to investigate the *Aurora* and to report on measures
to be taken against its editor.

Without any hearing, Duane was condemned by the committee and found guilty of 'seditious utterance.' The Senate
ordered him to appear before it on 24 March to defend him-

self. Duane appeared and requested counsel. He was told he could have counsel, but only for the purpose of denying the charges or in excusing them.

Duane's two lawyers refused to appear for him thus gagged. Accordingly Duane refused to appear on 26 March and the Senate promptly found him guilty of contempt. Duane evaded the Senate process server until adjournment.

In a parting shot at the defiant editor, the Senate asked the Adams administration to prosecute him for violation of the Sedition Law. The President complied. He was indicted 17 October 1800. Numerous postponements of his trial were obtained. Thomas Jefferson discontinued the prosecution, which thus never came to trial. In order to lay the issue that the Senate had raised, however, Jefferson directed the Grand Jury to inquire into what law Duane might have violated by criticizing the Senate. The Grand Jury found no law against it and refused to find an indictment.

One hundred and fifteen years elapsed before another Senate committee undertook an investigation of a newspaper.

Smarting under the defeat of a Ship Subsidy bill in 1915, administration senators succeeded in voting a special committee to investigate and find out if influence had been exerted. The committee was headed by Senator T. J. Walsh, Democrat, of Montana. It summoned before it a principal newspaper foe of the bill, the editor of the *New York Times*. In a long interrogation, the *New York Times* was put on trial for its opinions.[10] The editor, Charles Ransom Miller, was then asked if the paper had any financial support from abroad, particularly from England. The *New York Times* said editorially:

This is not a personal issue. It is a question of the extent to which a government's machinery may be privately misused to annoy and attempt to discredit a newspaper whose editorial attitude has become distasteful and embarrassing.[11]

At the conclusion of his testimony the *Times* editor said:

I can see no ethical, moral, or legal right that you have to put many of the questions you put to me today. Inquisitorial proceedings of this kind would have a very marked tendency, if continued and adopted as a policy, to reduce the press of the United States to the level of the press in some of the Central European empires, the press that has been known as the reptile press, that crawls on its belly every day to the foreign office or to the government officials and ministers to know what it may say or shall say — to receive its orders.

He protested that such questions tended 'to repress freedom of utterance and to put newspapers under a sort of duress.'

## The Issue in 1936

A Senate committee investigating lobbying raised issues similar to those in the *New York Times* case in 1936. The committee, it was learned, had obtained from the Federal Communications Commission telegrams and press messages of some newspapers, including a message from William Randolph Hearst to one of his editorial writers.

Hearst tried to enjoin the FCC from giving up copies of messages and to enjoin the committee. He did not succeed in getting an injunction against the FCC because the courts of the District of Columbia held the act already had taken place, but they acknowledged that if 'the bill had been filed while the trespass was in process, it would have been the duty of the lower court, by order on the Commission or telegraph companies or the agents of the Committee to enjoin the acts complained of.' This opinion, by Justice J. Groner of the United States Court of Appeals for the District of Columbia, in a sense vindicated Hearst's complaint of wrongdoing, although it gave him no legal redress.

At the same time, the Court held that it could not restrain the Senate committee from making use of the telegrams it had already obtained because the courts 'cannot enjoin legislative debate or discussion of constitutional measures because of the incidental disclosure or publication of knowledge unconstitutionally acquired.'

The citizens' remedy for the abuse of legislative power, the Court said, must be of another sort. In the case of improper questions, it pointed out, the witness 'would be entitled to refuse to answer; and if, for his supposed contumacy, he were imprisoned, he could secure his release on habeas corpus.'

In other words, the citizen cannot restrain the Congress from exercise of unconstitutional or illegal power, but can only defy the Congress and go to the courts to escape punishment for his defiance, taking the chance that he may be mistaken as to the rights of the committee.

A clearer case of the use of congressional power to punish utterance came in April 1936. Frank C. Waldrop wrote an article in the *Washington Herald*, published on 3 April 1936, connecting Representative John J. McSwain of the House Committee on Military Affairs with some war surplus speculators. McSwain had Waldrop subpoenaed to appear on 6 April before his committee. When the committee met to hear Waldrop, his attorney said the committee was proceeding improperly 'pursuant to a threat of its chairman and without legislative purpose, and that his client would answer no questions.' Waldrop refused to answer all questions, declining even to give his name. He was asked to stand down but hold himself subject to recall. Then the committee examined other witnesses until 15 April when it voted unanimously to end its inquiry, not to print the record of its proceedings, and to make no report to the House. Waldrop's counsel asked and obtained cancellation of the subpoena.

### The Rumely Case

The Rumely case, decided by the United States Supreme Court 9 March 1953, resulted in several concurring opinions which dealt extensively with the power of Congress to harass the press or visit upon it reprisal for publication.

In 1949, Edward A. Rumely, as secretary of an organization known as the Committee on Constitutional Government, was called before the Lobbying Committee of the House. He re-

fused to give the names of persons who had purchased books
from his organization. He was cited for contempt. He was
found guilty of contempt by the United States District Court,
District of Columbia. The United States Court of Appeals
reversed the judgment and remanded the case with instructions
to dismiss. The reversal was on two grounds.

The Court held that to publicize the names would be 'a
realistic interference with the publication and sale of those
writings.' It concluded that 'the realistic effect of public embarrassment is a powerful interference with the free expression
of views.' It further said that the sale of books was not 'lobbying,' which the committee was authorized to investigate,
and therefore outside the jurisdiction and authority of the
committee.

The United States Supreme Court affirmed this reversal.
The majority opinion, written by Justice Felix Frankfurter,
held simply that the committee was without power to do more
than investigate lobbying and that Rumely's activities did not
constitute lobbying.

A concurring opinion by Justice William Douglas and Justice Hugo Black took up the constitutional questions involved.
It stated:

Of necessity I come then to the constitutional questions. Respondent
(Rumely) represents a segment of the American press. Some may
like what his group publishes; others may disapprove. These tracts
may be the essence of wisdom to some; to others their point of view
and philosophy may be anathema. To some ears their words may be
harsh and repulsive; to others they may carry the hope of the future.
We have here a publisher who through books and pamphlets seeks
to reach the minds and hearts of the American people. He is different
in some respects from other publishers. But the differences are
minor. Like the publishers of newspapers, magazines or books, this
publisher bids for the minds of men in the market place of ideas.
The aim of the historic struggle for a free press was to 'establish
and preserve the right of the English people to full information in
respect of the doings or misdoings of their government' (Gros-
jean *v.* American Press Col, 297 US 233,247). That is the tradition
behind the First Amendment. Censorship or previous restraint is

banned (Near *v.* Minn., 283 US 697). The privilege of pamphleteer-ing, as well as the more orthodox types of publications may neither be licensed (Lovell *v.* Griffin, 303 US 444) nor taxed (Murdock *v.* Penn., 319 US 105). Door to door distribution is privileged (Mar-tin *v.* Struthers, 319 US 141). These are illustrative of the pre-ferred position granted speech and the press by the First Amend-ment. The command that 'Congress shall make no law . . . abridging the freedom of speech or of the press' has behind it a long history. It expresses the confidence that the safety of society depends on tolerance of government for hostile as well as friendly criticism, that in a community where men's minds are free, there must be room for the unorthodox as well as the orthodox views.

If the present inquiry were sanctioned the press would be sub-jected to harassment that in practical effect might be as serious as censorship. A publisher, compelled to register with the federal government would be subjected to harassing inquiries. A require-ment that a publisher disclose the identity of those who buy his books, pamphlets, or paper is indeed the beginning of surveillance of the press. True, no legal sanction is involved here. Congress has imposed no tax, established no board of censors, instituted no licensing system. But the potential restraint is equally severe. The finger of government levelled against the press is ominous. Once the government can demand of a publisher the names of the purchasers of his publications, the free press as we know it dis-appears. Then the spectre of a government agent will look over the shoulder of everyone who reads. The purchase of a book or pamphlet may result in a subpoena tomorrow. Fear of criticism goes with every person into the bookstall. The subtle, imponder-able pressures of the orthodox lay hold. Some will fear to read what is unpopular, what the powers-that-be dislike. When the light of publicity may reach any student, any teacher, inquiry will be discouraged. The books and pamphlets critical of the adminis-tration that preach an unpopular policy in domestic or foreign af-fairs, that are in disrepute in the orthodox school of thought will be suspect and subject to investigation. The press and its readers will pay a heavy price in harassment. But that will be minor in comparison with the menace of the shadow which government will cast over literature that does not follow the dominant party line. . . . Through the harassment of hearings, investigations, reports and subpoena government will hold a club over speech and over the press. Congress could not do this by law. The power of in-vestigation also is limited. Inquiry into personal and private affairs is precluded . . . And so is any matter in respect to which no valid legislation could be had . . . Since Congress could not by law require of respondent (Rumely) what the House demanded, it may not take the first step in an inquiry ending in fine or imprisonment.

It took an expensive four-year battle to find that the Buchanan Committee had no right to harass Rumely. Other citizens, in like position, still have no better redress against excesses of committee zeal.

## The Wechsler Case

On 24 April 1953, James Wechsler, editor of the *New York Post*, was called before the Senate Committee on Government Operations. Mr. Wechsler had long been a vigorous critic of the members of this committee and of other congressional investigating committees.

He was first questioned about books that he had written. Then he was asked many questions about the editorial policies of the *New York Post*. He was asked about various editorials critical of congressional investigations, in nearly all of which there were references to the chairman of the committee, Senator Joseph McCarthy of Wisconsin.

Wechsler, unlike Waldrop or Rumely, answered the questions he was asked, acknowledged his one-time association with the Communist party, his brief membership, and gave the names of others he knew in the party at that time.

Although he submitted to the interrogation, he felt that the committee was infringing upon the constitutional guaranties of a free press and attempting to intimidate newspapers that might be inclined to criticize congressional committees, as the *Post* had done.

He appealed to the Freedom of Information Committee of the American Society of Newspaper Editors to support him in this contention. This committee made a divided report. It asked for independent legal study of the questions raised to find out if editors, under these circumstances, ought to answer questions or refuse to answer them.

Four of the eleven members of the committee felt more strongly. They concluded that:

(1) Freedom of the Press in these United States, as it has been understood since the adoption of the Constitution, could not long survive the repeated exercise by Congress of unlimited inquiry into the conduct of newspapers.

(2) Congressional interrogation, such as occurred in the United States Senate Committee on April 24 and May 5, if frequently repeated, would extinguish, without the passage of a single law, that free and unfettered reporting of events and comment thereon, upon which the preservation of our liberties depends, for more is comprehended in the term 'freedom of the press' than just immunity to punitive statutes, it having been the intent of the founding fathers to free the press from all restraints and harassment by government.

(3) Newspapers put to the necessity of explaining to government agencies, legislative or executive, their news and editorial policies, under oath, would exist in such permanent jeopardy that their freedom to report fully and comment freely inevitably would be impaired. They would exist under an intimidation and harassment wholly incompatible with American ideas of liberty. A press that is under the continuing necessity of accounting to government for its opinions is not a free press — whether the government be a good or bad government. A press put to the frequent necessity of explaining its news and editorial policies to a United States senator, armed with the full powers of the government of the United States is not a free press — whether the Senator be a good or bad senator.

### The 1955 Cases

The Senate Internal Security Subcommittee, in July 1955, questioned several newspapermen on past Communist Party affiliations.

At one point these interrogations definitely took on the shape of harassment and punishment for publication of news reports that the committee disliked. Charles Grutzner, of the *New York Times*, was sharply questioned about stories of disorderly behavior by United States Army personnel in Korea and his interrogators meaningfully asserted his stories had been picked up by the Communist New York *Daily Worker*. His news reports on the first Sabre jet encounters in Korea were the subject of interrogation implying and asserting that these reports had betrayed military secrets to the enemy.

Reporters, working under the knowledge that their written work, if displeasing to some Senate committee, may bring them before a committee under subpoena to explain their reports, might easily be intimidated by this knowledge. This kind of reprisal for publication, whether or not intended as reprisal, makes the free expression of opinion and the honest reporting of events politically hazardous.

### Intimidation

The test of the damage done by congressional reprisal is not alone the reaction of interrogated and questioned editors and reporters to the ordeal of their inquisitions.

James Wechsler denied that he had been intimidated. It is doubtful that the *New York Times* has been intimidated. This is not the full test, however.

The effect of the hearings upon the press generally is the thing about which the people must be concerned. They are dependent for their information upon the free operation of all publications — not just upon the uninterrupted operations of those owned by the most resourceful and most courageous managements.

Editors directly involved may not be intimidated. Other editors, less strongly situated or less courageous, may be intimidated by the very example of interrogation they witness.

John Lilburne, arrested for publishing seditious pamphlets, in 1637, was tried by star chamber, sentenced in its secret proceedings, lashed to the tail of a cart, whipped across London, put in the pillory, and imprisoned. During his ordeal he exhorted the crowds along the line of march. He cried out his opinions. He scattered pamphlets. He continued to shout when put in the pillory. He was gagged, and he stamped his feet and shook his head and gesticulated to show that if he could do so, he would still speak. He was thrown in a dungeon and loaded with irons. This did not intimidate him, evidently, because in 1639 he was still stoutly proclaiming his views and was, in that year, put on trial for treason. He was not intimidated, but no one knows how many other Englishmen, of lesser stuff, who watched his awful ordeal were intimidated. If only that intimidation that is successful against those who are the immediate object of its violence is held to be iniquitous, we must prepare to allow tyranny much more license than free people hitherto have conceded to it.

No newspapers in the United States have been closed by congressional committees (as were some in Argentina). Perhaps none will be closed. If all utterance that is critical of government results in public interrogation, under the compulsion of arrest and subpoena, or the threat of it, it is folly to suppose that such criticism will not be checked. The newspapers may still be printed, but they will cease to perform, in all but a few cases, the purposes of a free press. To whatever degree any of them, out of the fear of what a committee may say or do to them under the sanction of congressional authority, desist from criticism of authority, to that degree the American people will have lost the right to know.

### Reprisal by the Mob

The press must be secure not only against the reprisal and intervention of government. It also must be secure against reprisal by lawless persons operating in disregard of the laws, in defiance of government or under the encouragement of government.

Benjamin Bache, editor of the *Aurora* of Philadelphia, was one of the first to suffer this kind of reprisal as he was one of the first to suffer reprisal by government, under the Constitution.[12] Federalist newspapers were so incensed by his support of France that they urged businessmen to withdraw advertising from Bache. His advertising revenue and his circulation suffered. In 1798 his house was twice attacked by mobs and he was personally assaulted. Later a mob smashed the windows of his home. He was assaulted by Abel Humphreys and by John Ward Fenno.

A rival newspaper urged tar and feathers for another Republican editor, John Daly Burk of the New York *Timepiece*.[13]

Editors have been threatened with violence in many other turbulent periods of American history.

The murder of Elijah Lovejoy, on 7 November 1837, is the foremost American example of mob reprisal for the expression of opinion, carried out under the sanction of preponderant opinion in the community, in defiance of and with some co-operation by authority.

The editor of the Alton, Illinois, paper had outraged pro-slavery sentiment in his area. A mob burst into the warehouse where his press was in storage (after previous presses had been thrown in the river) and killed Lovejoy. Those who had tried to defend him were subsequently indicted by a grand jury because they 'resisted and opposed with force and arms, violently and tumultuously and unlawfully, an attempt of certain persons, unknown, to break up and destroy a printing press, the property of said defendant.'

The dead editor's associates were acquitted. When the leaders of the mob finally were indicted, however, they also were acquitted.

Violence of this kind made the expression of sentiments at variance with those of the community dangerous in many areas of the United States during the years preceding the Civil War.

In some communities, in more recent years, it has been dangerous to report facts and express opinions. Don Mellett, the editor of the *Canton Repository*, was murdered on 16 July 1926 by a thug employed by the Ohio underworld to put a stop to the newspaper's disclosures.

These isolated reprisals may occur from time to time in even the most orderly society.

In 1939, the Federal Court at Mobile, Alabama, dealt with another type of reprisal and intimidation by the mob. On 6 May of that year, it found five people guilty of trapping and

photographing an editor in a compromising position in order
to silence his attacks on the local underworld. The government prosecutor said that the defendants had conspired to
intimidate Henry P. Ewald, former executive editor of the
*Mobile Press Register*, who was conducting a campaign against
gambling. Ewald was photographed and beaten. The indictments were brought under Title 18, Section 51 of the United
States Code which prohibits conspiracy to intimidate 'any
citizens in the free exercise of . . . or enjoyment of any
right or privilege secured to him by the Constitution of the
United States.'

This section of the code is not often employed against reprisal of this sort and probably should be invoked more frequently where even the threat of combinations for the purpose of intimidation can be discerned.

Where this kind of violence and reprisal can be threatened
with impunity, by individuals or groups of individuals seeking
to enforce their views upon other citizens, the community, of
course, will not have access to nonconforming opinion or
facts at variance with the wishes of the preponderating sentiment of a community.

Violence of this kind was utilized by the government of
Argentina to destroy *La Prensa*, the great liberal daily of
Buenos Aires. Mobs were set upon the newspaper to prevent
its continued publication and were permitted to interfere
with its operations without intervention by the police.[14]

The futility of theoretical freedom in the face of threats
of this sort has been quaintly illustrated by a story related by
Zechariah Chafee, Jr., and which he quoted from Galsworthy:

The other day in Russia an Englishman came on a street-meeting
shortly after the first revolution had begun. An extremist was addressing the gathering and telling them that they were fools to go
on fighting, that they ought to refuse and go home, and so forth.
The crowd grew angry, and some soldiers were for making a rush
at him; but the chairman, a big burly peasant, stopped them with
these words: 'Brothers, you know that our country is now a country of free speech. We must listen to this man, we must let him

say anything he will. But, brothers, when he's finished, we'll bash his head in.' [15]

Freedom of speech that can be exercised only at the risk of a broken head does not amount to much. There must be immunity from reprisal for lawful utterance and the penalties for even wrongful publication must not be such that the penalties for casual, incidental, or unintended error are fatal.

Citizens must not only be left free from government penalties and mob reprisals for reporting what they know about government and commenting on it; they must be encouraged to exercise such freedoms and permitted to enjoy the rewards of popular support if they merit it, or win it.

Nor is it enough for a free government merely to curtail, diminish, and restrain the influences that make free reporting of facts and free expression of opinion hazardous. The requirements of freedom are not satisfied in a climate where only the rich, powerful, resourceful, and courageous dare assert the right to utter what is unpopular. There must be encouragement, in an affirmative way, for those who seek knowledge and desire to use it. The indifference, indolence, and ignorance of great numbers of citizens will be a serious barrier to the full realization of mankind's greatness. Where the state is hostile and the population prejudiced against freedom of expression, this freedom and every other freedom will not long survive. Where reprisal against utterance, however hateful, is sponsored by the state or tolerated by the people, citizens will not know enough about their government, or about the life around them, to discharge the responsibilities imposed upon them in a democratic society.

# 8

---

## The Right Of Access To The Means Of Publishing

*To admit that the state can determine the assignment of printing materials that are indispensable for daily papers, such as newsprint, is the same as admitting that freedom of the press is at the mercy of simple economic measures that are at best debatable.* — LA PRENSA *

FREEDOM of the press exists in theory in a society where citizens have a right to get information, and a right to print it without prior restraint or unwarranted punishment subsequent to publication.

The right which thus exists in theory will not exist in fact, however, if to these constitutional rights there is not added the practical right of access to the instruments of publication. Secrecy about government may still prevail, and silence about nongovernmental affairs still may be enforced, if citizens cannot obtain the use of the facilities of publication.

Private persons must be able to buy presses (or the use of them), paper (or the use of it), radio and television stations

* 5 March 1946.

(or the use of them), and public halls and meeting places (or the use of them), without the interposition of governmental power if the ideal enjoyment of the liberty of utterance is to be afforded. The law must permit them to do it, and the economic means of doing it must not be such that the right is limited to and reserved for only a privileged few in society.

How do we stand on this fourth freedom?

### Access to Presses

Government, in the United States, does not limit the right of citizens to buy, own, or rent presses. Congress has taken one step toward this infringement on the freedom to print by passing a law requiring the registration of printing equipment used by Communist-front organizations, but even this statute does not prevent or forbid the Communist organizations the use of printing presses. The statute is objectionable as a first step toward limiting access to presses.

In at least one state, the right to own a press is so highly regarded that the owners of newspaper presses are especially protected by law against the foreclosure of mortgages on presses.

The complete control of all printing equipment, in Communist countries, is the clinching device for the absolute suppression of anything offensive to government and the culminating instrument for maintaining secrecy in all things except those that the state wishes to have published.

The great cost of printing machinery used in publications of general circulation makes such facilities quite out of the reach of the ordinary citizen, even in the United States where there are no political barriers to the purchase of a press. From the standpoint of a citizen wishing to start a newspaper, things were more favorable in a day when the Washington Hand Press and a few fonts of type constituted the basic physical equipment of a newspaper. Even then, of course, these means of publication must have been beyond the reach of most citizens. Colonial statesmen certainly never contemplated a society in which each and every citizen had his own press and surely never believed this essential to free utterance. Yet, ideally, the readier access to printing machinery that there is for the ordinary man, the safer the freedom of the press is, and the more secure society is against secrecy in public affairs. It is easier for government as such to operate against a few great presses than it is for it to control great numbers of small presses. The vulnerability of large printing establishments to arbitrary political control was well demonstrated when the Nazi invaders moved into the countries of free Europe. It was easy for them to stop the big printing plants, but it proved nearly impossible to choke off the free press that sprang into being everywhere. So we cannot be unconcerned over the problems raised by the possession of printing equipment by a relatively few persons. A free people will feel most secure where there are no political barriers to the ownership of printing facilities and where the economic barriers are not such as to discourage their ownership by citizens generally.

## Radio and Television

Radio and television facilities are less available, both politically and economically, than the facilities of publication.

The federal licensing of radio and television stations, imposed by the mechanical exigencies arising out of a limited number of wave lengths, is inconsistent with the principles of the First Amendment. No one has come forward with any proposal by which this can be escaped. It is a limitation on free utterance, the elimination of which ought to be the object of all our scientific ingenuity if we wish to gain for this sort of communication the immunity to political interference that has been the chief virtue of our press.

The financial obstacles to radio and television station ownership are also very great.

## Alternatives to Ownership

The obstacles to ownership make even more important the alternative to ownership, which is the ability to rent or use the facilities of publication.

Whatever differences there are between our society and that of the colonial period in which our ideas on freedom of the press were developed, they probably are differences more of degree than of kind. Freedom of speech was not really conferred, in equal measure, upon all citizens when the First Amendment was adopted. The man who owned a stump had some practical advantage over his stumpless fellow citizens. The man with a meeting house was better off than the homeless wanderer. The man with a few fonts of type and a press had readier access to the printed word than his fellows.

The founding fathers did not attempt to eliminate the disparities arising out of these economic differences. It was their faith that private citizens, freed from restraints by government and protected against the unlawful interference of their fellows, would find out the truth and make it known. Interference by government was the evil with which they had had most experience. It was freedom *from* government that they were attempting to secure.

Citizens of that day, like the citizens of today, derived benefits from press freedom without themselves owning printing plants or running newspapers. They derived their chief benefits as readers of the press through which they got the facts upon which they based their opinions. They also, however, had access to the press for the expression of their own opinions and judgments. Early newspapers often were primarily collections of letters written by citizens who did not share at all in the ownership of the publications for which they wrote. The early newspaper owners sometimes were more printers than editors and often were glad to have the offerings of more gifted writers.

Benjamin Franklin, in the long years when he represented Pennsylvania in England, made great use of the English newspapers. His letters appeared in literally dozens of publications. Later, when he was the representative of his country in France, he continued to furnish the press with letters, and newspapers in France and on the continent carried his letters under various pseudonyms.

The letter to the editor still is a means by which an ordinary citizen can gain use of the columns of a newspaper that he does not own. It is a by-no-means contemptible device today, any more than it was in colonial times.

The letter columns of great metropolitan newspapers today carry the contributions of citizens and statesmen, of persons in every level of society and of every shade of political belief. In spite of all the pressure for space that is felt in modern newspaper offices, it is doubtful that a propagandist of the skill of Ben Franklin would have any more difficulty now than he had then in getting his opinions before the audience he wished to reach. In this respect, at least, it is no more difficult (if it is as difficult) to 'rent' a newspaper. The citizen with a cause to cry or a complaint to make, if he is responsible, can usually get his letter printed. If he is the representative of, or the spokesman for, any considerable number of his fellows, his task is even easier.

An even more common way of 'renting' a newspaper is that utilized every day by public figures with names that make news. Few newspapers close their columns to interesting utterance by persons of all political beliefs. They seldom print at length (or at least at as great a length as speakers would wish) the remarks of orators of the day. But the substance of what is said does get reported, usually without regard to editors' views on it.

For those who cannot get into the letter columns or the news columns, and for those who want to have more control over the manner in which what they wish to say is treated, there is an alternative that is coming into wider use. The editorial advertisement now furnishes another way in which the average citizen can rent a piece of a newspaper.

More and more frequently individual, private companies and unions and associations are buying space at advertising rates in which to present facts, arguments, and opinions which they wish to lay before newspaper readers. Daily newspapers, in many cities, are carrying hundreds of thousands of lines of such editorial advertising each year.

Newspapers, of course, do not have to accept this advertising. The right to print comprehends the right not to print. Most of them, however, feel a strong compulsion to print controversial editorial material, irrespective of their own views on it, if it conforms to standards to which the newspapers themselves are compelled to adhere in the regulation of the content of their own news and editorial columns.

While there may be no legal compulsion to do so, there are strong ethical and practical compulsions to make advertising columns available to responsible advertisers. This is a very practical means of rendering less onerous and objectionable the practical restrictions on the extent of actual newspaper ownership. Those who find it fairly easy and convenient to use newspaper columns when they wish to employ them, are likely to have their own participation in the benefits of press freedom widened. When newspaper columns are open to all, freedom of the press becomes a right more meaningful to rank-and-file citizens.

Yet, newspapers cannot yield up column inches of white paper without any strings attached. In the eighteenth century it was sometimes argued that, ideally, printers ought to be viewed as common carriers; that writers only ought to be responsible for material that was libelous, scandalous, or defamatory. This view, however, did not get into our statutes relating to the press. The newspaper is free — but it is also responsible. So the same limits that the law puts on a newspaper, the newspaper must put upon its advertisers. Many advertisers find this restraint offensive and regard it as an infringement upon their enjoyment of press freedom. Sometimes they offer to assume financial responsibility for ensuing litigation. Even this does not relieve a newspaper of its own responsibility. It is obliged, legally and morally, to refuse much advertising.

Some of the grounds for refusing copy are perfectly clear. A newspaper must not publish that which is libelous, scandalous, defamatory, obscene, lewd, or immoral. It can hardly allow an advertiser to advocate illegal action, such as boycotts, riots, tax evasion, draft evasion, arson, assault, or other crimes. It certainly should not permit the use of its space to perpetrate fraud. It cannot permit an advertiser to defame the products of another person. It surely cannot allow advertisers to publish demonstrated falsehoods about events that have taken place, for the purpose of misleading citizens. It cannot countenance advertisements for which the advertiser will not assume responsibility, which he will not sign or underwrite.

Some would-be editorial advertisers find such standards inhibiting. To protect themselves against such offenses, newspapers must exercise a form of prior restraint and censorship on advertising copy. It is difficult to see how it can be avoided without sweeping changes in our statutes that would relieve the press of all responsibility for this sort of utterance. Until this happens, newspapers certainly will have to make certain that what their advertisers say does not violate the law or the canons of good taste.

The editorial advertiser, within these limits, enjoys access to printing facilities on convenient terms. He has available not only the equipment of the newspaper but the 'loan' of its audience.

The right 'not to print' is an aspect of press freedom, but it cannot be invoked in violation of other rights. When used to enforce discrimination or to suppress competition, it is subject to government scrutiny.

The Lorain Journal Company of Lorain, Ohio, in September 1949 was accused by the government of conspiring to monopolize the spread of news and advertising by refusing to accept the advertising of firms who placed advertising with competing radio stations and in a competing newspaper. In August 1950, Judge Emerich B. Freed, of the federal court at Cleveland, found the newspaper 'guilty of attempting to establish a monopoly by bold, relentless, predatory commercial behavior.' The United States Supreme Court, on 11 December 1951, affirmed the opinion of the lower court and enjoined the newspaper to refrain from the complained-of practices (Lorain Journal Company v. United States, Official Reports of The Supreme Court, Volume 342, U.S. Number 2, p. 143).

In testimony before the House Small Business Committee on 16 November 1955, Assistant Attorney General Stanley N. Barnes pointed out that access to advertising columns of newspapers and magazines is necessary to 'free competition in open markets.' The Department of Justice, during the same week, filed an antitrust suit against a group of makers of telescopic rifle sights and outdoor magazine publishers because the magazines denied advertising space to certain dealers.

The 'right not to print' undoubtedly would be upheld when invoked in most cases, but government and the courts, it is plain, are beginning to assert a corresponding right of citizens to gain access to the advertising columns of publications where the denial of that right can be identified with an effort to compel economic discrimination.

### The Problem of Newsprint

Availability of printing materials is essential to public information, too.

Political devices for interfering with the supply of newsprint are almost as old as newsprint itself. England restricted the size of newspapers until 1825. Shortages growing out of wartime compelled similar restrictions from the start of World War II. A stamp duty on newspaper supplements was enforced in England until 1855. Paper duties were not repealed until 1861.[1]

The way political control of newsprint and politically motivated taxes on newsprint can be used to crush a free newspaper has been demonstrated very clearly in Argentina.[2]

For decades, newsprint had entered Argentina without duty, but on 31 October 1946, five months after Peron came into power, it was alleged by his customs officers that the opposition newspapers *La Prensa* and *La Nación* had evaded taxes on that portion of their newsprint used to print advertising, which was held to be taxable. After years of litigation, in 1951, after *La Prensa* had been closed, the government held that it was owed 32,038,391 pesos in such taxes.[3]

In 1945 the government began expropriating the newsprint stocks of *La Prensa*, and also disclosed its intention to seize 10 per cent of all *La Prensa*'s newsprint imports. In July 1947, the Central Bank suspended the issuance of exchange permits for the importation of newsprint. Finally the government ordered *La Prensa* to cut its editions from an average of thirty-two pages to sixteen pages.[4]

Newsprint control (in the face of limited supplies) was managed in the United States during wartime restrictions and for a longer period in Great Britain, without any serious allegations of political abuses. The danger of political control exists, however, wherever the supply of newsprint is dependent upon government. Wherever newsprint is dutiable there is always the danger that a corrupt government may use the construction of the tariff schedules to punish unfriendly newspapers and favor friendly newspapers. Freedom of the press is most secure against this threat where newsprint moves with utter freedom across national boundaries, without any political control whatever.

## Newsprint Economics

Removing all political controls does not entirely solve the problem of newsprint. The importance of an abundant newsprint supply is well stated in *Paper for Printing*, published by UNESCO in 1952. This publication said:

A sufficiency of newsprint, available at a fair price is necessary if a vigorous press is to give a balanced diet of home and world news, cultural and scientific features, sport, entertainment and advertising. Whenever newspapers are so seriously cramped for lack of reasonably priced paper as in many countries they have been for years, the less desirable news items, for which the demand is greatest, almost invariably encroach upon space formerly taken up by foreign affairs, culture and science, while the proportion of space devoted to advertising tends to be maintained so that heavy losses of advertising revenue are avoided. . . It is generally true to say that the greater the supply of newsprint, the greater are the opportunities for making newspapers informative, intelligent and universal in appeal, just as the shrinkage of newspapers is usually associated with insufficient news coverage and a consequent decline in quality. In present circumstances of newsprint scarcity combined with high and wildly fluctuating newsprint prices, many newspapers in many countries fall a long way behind the standards achieved before the second world war.[5]

There is not an 'abundant supply of newsprint at a fair price' today, any more than there was in 1952. What is even more distressing to those who realize the importance of newsprint to freedom of the press, there is not likely to be an abundant supply at a fair price in the near future.

The supply that does exist in the world is most unequally distributed. The world average supply per capita in 1952 was 8.37 pounds. The United States consumed 79.36 pounds per capita. Europe got 11.9 pounds; South America 15.4 pounds; Asia less than one-half pound. In many parts of the world, the press cannot perform its functions with the existing tonnage of newsprint available. Whole vast areas of government and private transactions remain 'secret' so far as citizens are concerned, because there simply is not enough newsprint on which to report what is happening.

The 1952 UNESCO study estimated that by 1960, if present trends of production and consumption continue, world demand will exceed world supply by between 3.6 million and 4.6 million tons, or by 39 to 50 per cent.[6]

Price, in many areas of the world, is a limiting factor almost as serious as the supply. Newsprint cost $46 a ton in 1933. It rose to $126 in 1955 and in the latter months of that year to

$131. Such increases in price compel many newspapers to curtail the total amount of newsprint devoted to the publication of news and opinion. Information about government, business, and society in general, that would be printed if newsprint prices were lower, simply goes unreported. The pressure of this unseen, economic 'censorship' is felt in every newspaper office. Services to readers are curtailed on the one hand, diminishing the amount of information given subscribers; circulation prices are increased on the other hand, tending to diminish the number of newspaper readers. Both trends operate to curtail the people's knowledge and information.

There seems to be little occasion to hope that enough additional newsprint factories can be built, or will be built, to maintain adequate supplies of newsprint and to accommodate the increases that ought to occur in countries already seriously undersupplied. As the gap between supply and demand increases, quotas and rationing, with all attendant possibilities of political manipulation and control, may become even more necessary in many countries.

## Newspaper Competition

Steadily diminishing daily newspaper competition has caused many to fear that the means of expression may become less and less available to citizens.

The number of daily newspapers in the United States declined from 2,202 in 1909–10 to 1,760 in 1953–54. The number of cities with competing daily newspapers declined from 689 to only 87. The number of cities with non-competing dailies increased from 518 to 1,361. Eighteen states are now without any locally competing daily newspapers.[7]

Obviously, this contraction is not as serious as it would be in a country with a party press, such as Denmark, which for decades had the four-party paper system with each political party having its newspaper voice in Copenhagen and in the provinces.[8]

Nor is it quite as serious as it would have been in an earlier period when most American daily newspapers were the voices of political parties.

The disappearance of competition is nonetheless disquieting.

This noncompetitive situation puts it within the power of the monopoly newspaper to suppress facts at its discretion, many people fear.

Actually, the risk is diminished by (1) the degree to which newspaper circulations overlap, thereby threatening the suppressing newspaper with disclosure; (2) the growing competition between the monopoly newspaper and such media as radio and television; and (3) the steadily increasing competition between the newspaper and the periodical press.

So far as major national news is concerned, and perhaps to some extent even so far as important state news is concerned, no local newspaper really enjoys an effective monopoly. It cannot withhold from its readers substantial news (which it may find offensive to its policies), even if it wishes to do so, without exposing itself to public reproach and criticism. And notwithstanding the trend to fewer daily newspapers, this reproach and criticism can reach a point where disgruntled customers will take steps to start a rival newspaper.

The danger of secrecy for unpalatable facts is greater in the area of local news. In this area of the news, the facts involved may be known only to the newsgathering staff of the local newspapers. In these cases, its discretion is great and its fear of detection diminished.

Few critics of newspapers can furnish many examples of real abuse of power of this kind, however. This circumstance probably is less a tribute to the morality of monopoly newspaper ownership than it is to the nature of the newspaper profession. It is difficult to attract and keep competent newspaper craftsmen in a newspaper institution that habitually violates the inborn professional spirit of newspapermen. The lifelong habit of getting and printing the news is not to be frustrated easily because of the passing whim of ownership.

This sort of immorality gains the contempt of the profession to a degree probably not wholly understood by others. The most callous managements are not wholly indifferent to reproach for such irregularities.

Deliberate conspiracy to withhold news disliked by a newspaper is probably far less common, or dangerous, than another sort of conspiracy — the conspiracy that springs from circumstances attending newspaper production. The lack of resources required to gather and to print the news probably inspires more suppression of information than the willful secrecy of newspaper management or staff. The rising costs of newspaper publication, running straight across all the means of production from newsprint to labor, frequently cause a curtailment of information service which imposes upon any management that can survive a kind of secrecy in regard to many phases of community life.

The clash of hostile opinion is also missed in newspaper monopoly cities. The most conscientious and responsible monopoly newspapers have tried hard to provide a substitute for the oldfashioned editorial page combat of an earlier period. They have opened their columns to factions of opposing views. They have purchased syndicated writers of different attitudes and conflicting political alignment. This sort of managed contest, however, lacks the fire and zeal of the editorial expressions of newspapers that used to compete for the minds of the readers in a city. Whatever the intentions of these competitive newspapers, in their urge to get the better of each other they ventilated public questions in an exciting and interesting way. There is no real substitute for this sort of clash. There was little chance that any political secrets would survive this sort of competition.

The more that newspaper competition disappears, the more we tend to forget that it had some disadvantages to society, too. Conflict in print sometimes inflamed opposing factions just when their differences should have been composed. In the scramble for circulation, political support, and advertising, partisan newspapers sometimes were led into exaggerations, extravagant assertions, downright falsehood, and sheer sensationalism. The sheer number of newspapers a hundred years ago condemned most of them to marginal operations, in which owners were often open to temptations that do not assail more prosperous monopoly newspapers.

Alexis de Tocqueville has described some of the disadvantages of the abundant newspaper competition that once existed in America in the 1830's.

> The facility with which newspapers can be established produces a multitude of them; but as the competition prevents any considerable profit, persons of much capacity are rarely led to engage in these undertakings. Such is the number of the public prints that even if they were a source of wealth, writers of ability could not be found to direct them all. The journalists of the United States are generally in a very humble position, with a scanty education and a vulgar turn of mind. . . The characteristics of the American journalist consist in an open and coarse appeal to the passions of his readers; he abandons principles to assail the characters of individuals, to track them into private life and disclose all their weaknesses and vices.[9]

Many who clamor for the 'good old days' of competitive journalism might be horrified at the kind of journalists and journalism that the 'good old days' would produce.

Despite the dangers of overcompetition, however, the virtues of some degree of competition have been hard to achieve under monopoly ownership. The existence of two or more newspapers in a city furnishes the public the only kind of a check on the press that is suitable in a democratic society — the check of one publication upon another. It has been difficult to devise a check that is as satisfactory which does not threaten the freedom of the press.

It is not remarkable that, under the circumstances of widespread monopoly ownership, citizens have become increasingly concerned over the possibility that this might mean that effective access to the press would be unavailable to some groups. This concern, of itself, is probably one of the best means of preventing monopoly from exhibiting its worst aspects. A free society must be constantly alert to see that its knowledge of affairs is not limited by either economic or political measures that deprive it of access to the means of publishing information that the laws have allowed it to acquire.

# 9

---

## The Right To Distribute

*And yet on the other hand unless wariness be used, as*
*good almost kill a Man as kill a good Book; who kills a*
*Man kills a reasonable creature, God's Image; but he who*
*destroys a good Book, kills reason itself, kills the Image*
*of God, as it were in the eye.* — MILTON, *Areopagitica.*

OF THAT whole process by which an idea is conveyed from the
mind of an author to the mind of an auditor, the act of distribution is the culminating step.

If it cannot be accomplished, the whole process fails. A
government that has allowed citizens to get information, to
print it without prior restraint, and to publish without fear or
intimidation, and to have access to the means of publishing,
can still stop the public from satisfying its curiosity. It can
still maintain such secrets as it chooses to keep, and it can still
keep the people in ignorance of the daily life about them
that lies beyond the reach of their own immediate and personal observation.

If the delivery of the printed work can be stopped, the whole
process that has gone before becomes just an enormous waste

of energy, ending in the accumulation of so much spoiled paper.

A government that intends this sort of interference in the machinery of mass communication, or proposes to allow its citizens to effect such intervention, might just as well play the tyrant from the beginning, except of course that there always is the hope that bad intentions may be circumvented.

The apparatus by which distribution of the printed word is accomplished in the United States is infinitely complicated and involved, and it is extremely sensitive to intervention by government or by private groups.

This apparatus includes purveyors of printed material all the way from the individual newspaper carrier to the United States Post Office. Telegraph, telephone, and radio facilities are part of it. Newsdealers, newsstand operators, book distributors and bookstore owners — an infinite variety of private persons and associations is engaged in these enterprises. The operations of this apparatus are pretty much taken for granted. The consumers of printed material of all kinds seldom question the nature or existence of the 'last man' to link them with the whole system of mass communication. When this link between the individual and the society about him does fail, the reaction is more one of surprise than anything else. The right of citizens to enjoy the benefits of the distribution of printed material is a right of which there is so little general consciousness that the trespass upon it is seldom recognized as any kind of infringement upon a right essential to a democratic society. What is even more serious is the likelihood that the citizen may not even know of some of the failures in this distribution system. He will be aware, to be sure, of general collapse or mass disruption of the smooth-flowing devices that keep him in touch with a limitless number of his sources of information. Isolated bits of the system may fail him, however, without any impact upon his consciousness. People are not much disturbed by the letters they never get — if they never discover that the letters were sent.

## The United States Mails

The United States mails constitute the most important part of the American system for the distribution of printed material and, at the same time, the part most vulnerable to interference by government itself.

'Use of the mails is almost as much a part of the right of free speech as the right to use our tongues,' Justice Holmes warned in 1922.[1]

Access to the mails is essential for hundreds of daily, weekly, and monthly publications and the only effective means of mass distribution for material published irregularly.

It is remarkable that a function of government so intimately related to the most cautiously guarded of all American liberties has been left with so little protection by Congress that the right to distribute can be withdrawn, to all practical effect, by administrative order at executive discretion.

The Institute of Legal Research of the Law School of the University of Pennsylvania has undertaken the first really extensive and complete analysis of the procedures by which citizens may be denied access to the mails. Such a study, it is to be hoped, will provoke a re-examination by the people and by Congress of their right to the mails. This re-examination surely will result in further protection against arbitrary refusal of the right than is afforded by present statutes.

Once the discretion to withhold the privilege of the mails is conceded, difficulties arise. The more closely this discretion can be confined, the safer citizens will be from whimsical and capricious denial of the mails. The very best of legislative efforts, however, must leave to administrative persons large areas of discretion within which to decide what is and what is not mailable. Safety, thereafter, lies in setting up procedures that surround this right with the same security citizens have against the imposition of prior restraint.

Even if the law is well devised, and discretion prevails in the Post Office Department, there always will be the risk that unjust exclusions are effected simply because the difficulties of asserting the right to the mails may be outside the resources of a litigant.

In other areas of our 'right to know' freedoms, government is concerned chiefly as a negative force against whose intervention the freedom of the press is to be defended. In the area of distribution, on the contrary, because of the enormous role of government itself, the right sought is an affirmative right. To make it effective we must be able to make the government do something — to accept for mailing and to deliver. This is, by its very nature, a more difficult thing. It is easier to restrain government than it is to compel it.

That mail tampering was a threat to press freedom was widely understood in days when the mails were less vital to the survival of publications than they are today.

In the period before the Civil War there were repeated efforts to ban abolition propaganda from the mails. In July 1835, the Charleston, South Carolina, post office was raided and abolitionist pamphlets burned. The postmaster at Charleston notified the New York postmaster to send no more such literature through the mails. The New York postmaster appealed to Postmaster General Amos Kendall, who announced that he would not direct New York to mail or require South Carolina to receive such materials.[2]

When Congress met the following December, President Andrew Jackson, in his message, complained of attempts to circulate through the mails 'inflammatory appeals addressed to the passions of the slaves' and asked for a law to 'prohibit under severe penalties the circulation in the southern states through the mail, of incendiary publications intended to instigate the slaves to insurrection.'

The President's suggestion was referred to a committee headed by John C. Calhoun, and the committee decided that it would be unconstitutional because Congress is commanded to make no law abridging the liberty of the press and a law forbidding the circulation of incendiary documents would imply the right of Congress to decide what papers may or may not be carried in the mails, and thereby subjects to its will and pleasure the freedom of the press on all subjects, moral, political, and religious.

Calhoun, who was as incensed by the pamphlets as the President, had another remedy. He would require postmasters to neither accept nor deliver such material only in the states where local laws had been passed against it, thus maintaining his constitutional theory as to federal power. After months of wrangling over the proposal it was defeated by a majority of six.[3] This Senate vote stopped an effort at government censorship of the mails for political reasons.

It did not stop all subsequent efforts in the same direction. Recently, several measures have been introduced under which material that advocated causes adjudged contrary to the interests of this country would be denied the mails.

Congress has been as cautious generally as it was in Calhoun's day in adopting laws expressly closing the mails to specified types of political opinion and information.

The Post Office Department, however, has been given broad statutory authority to declare some mail not acceptable for mailing and also to decide under what postal classifications matter is to be carried.

Under its authority to declare matter nonmailable, it can refuse the mails to publications that violate the Espionage Act or advocate treason, insurrection, or forcible resistance to any law of the United States. It can also refuse to accept matter that is 'obscene, lewd, or lascivious' and 'every filthy book, pamphlet, picture, paper, letter, writing, print or other publication of an indecent character.'

These statutes, in the language of Zechariah Chafee, Jr., 'make it possible for the Postmaster General and his subordinates to repress political thought in the name of loyalty and hamper literature and art in the name of decency.'[4]

The Post Office Department also can deny a second-class

mailing permit to a publication and make its circulation through the mails prohibitively costly. To be eligible for a second-class permit, a publication must: (1) be issued at stated intervals; (2) have a known office; (3) be printed; (4) be 'for the dissemination of information of a public character, or devoted to literature, the sciences, arts or some special industry'; (5) have a legitimate list of subscribers; and (6) be designed primarily for nonadvertising purposes.

In 1934, the Post Office Department, in denying a second-class mailing permit to *Esquire* magazine, held that the publication, in order to enjoy the permit, must 'contribute to the public good and the public welfare.'

Fortunately the United States Supreme Court did not agree with this standard. The risks of the 'public good' test of mailability were outlined by Justice Douglas, who said, in his opinion:

Under our system of government there is an accommodation for the widest varieties of tastes and ideas. What is good literature, what has educational value, what is refined public information, what is good art, varies with individuals as it does from one generation to another. There doubtless would be contrariety of views concerning Cervantes' *Don Quixote*, Shakespeare's *Venus and Adonis* and Zola's *Nana*. But a requirement that literature or art conform to some norm prescribed by an official smacks of an ideology foreign to our system. The basic values implicit in the requirements of the fourth condition can be served only by uncensored distribution of literature. From the multitude of competing offerings the public will pick and choose. What seems to one to be trash may have for others fleeting or even enduring values. But to withdraw the second-class rate from this publication today because its contents seemed to one official not good for the public would sanction withdrawal of the second-class rate tomorrow from another periodical whose social or economic views seemed harmful to another official.[5]

The dread 'tomorrow' which Justice Douglas feared seems already to have arrived so far as a great many publications printed abroad are concerned. Officials of the Treasury Department and of the Post Office Department acknowledged in 1955 that they have been holding up the delivery of alien publications that in the opinion of officials had subversive intent. Select delivery has been made to qualified research institutions, but the delivery through the mails of publications mailed abroad no longer is to be taken for granted.

These precautions, inferentially, confess a belief on the part of government that American citizens are susceptible to subversion by publication, notwithstanding every evidence that Communist doctrines have not been sufficiently attractive anywhere to overturn an existing government without the support of Soviet arms.

We have long deplored the iron curtain which has been thrown around Soviet Russia. We have justly regarded the refusal of the Communist government to admit any foreign publications as a mark of weakness and an indication of the government's lack of confidence in the reliability and loyalty of the people. It is only within the past year that Russia has admitted even the publications from friendly satellite regimes.

It is humiliating to think that post office and treasury officials have now made confessions of the same sort of doubts about the reliability and discretion of our citizens. This is a gross libel on the loyalty and dependability of Americans. There is not the slightest evidence that access to foreign literature has been dangerous to this country.

Those who framed the Constitution believed they had established a system the rightness of which would be only further illumined by new truths. So they did not fear truth. They believed the principles on which they had founded government so strong that that government never would be disturbed by falsehood. So they did not fear the dissemination of falsehood. Their judgment has been vindicated by 168 years of our history. We have even less occasion than our forefathers had to fear utterance or the printed word. Those who would keep Americans from seeing, hearing, or reading what they choose exhibit a lack of faith in the principles of our Bill of Rights and a lack of confidence in the people.

Many a military commander has scorched the earth ahead

of an invading army; but we are not so beset by literary Communist attacks on our principles that we need to scorch our freedoms in the face of foreign assaults upon them.

## The Post Office and Obscenity

In exercising its authority to exclude obscene matter from the mails, the present practice of the Post Office Department is to seize without prior notice or hearing mail regarded as obscene, to refer it to the solicitor of the Department, to then notify the mailer if the solicitor agrees that the matter is obscene, giving the mailer fifteen days to show cause why the objectionable matter should not be destroyed.

The sender is not given a hearing or permitted to refute or answer charges against his mailings. The power thus asserted is presumed to arise from Title 18, Section 1461 of the United States Code, but this statute does not expressly authorize this seizure and the powers have to be implied. Nevertheless, the Department has gone ahead on this theory of its powers, for eighty years, without any court decision on the doubtful issues raised.

During 1955, the Post Office Department seized a rare volume of Aristophanes' *Lysistrata* as obscene. When the mailer filed a suit to obtain an injunction to compel the return of the book, the Post Office Department returned it. Such challenges are rare and mailers generally acquiesce in the Department's rulings. Many are not able to finance a legal fight and others fear public reproach.

In 1950 Congress passed a new obscenity law under which, in addition to acting against the mail itself, the Department may cut off all mail addressed to the sender of the offensive material. This puts into the hands of post-office officials the power literally to destroy institutions on the complaint that they have improperly used the mails.

The sweeping authority the post-office officials have asserted is the more dangerous because of the difficulties of closely defining obscenity. It is hardly possible to draw up a rule on which any two citizens will agree exactly. Even persons long experienced in literary matters have difficulty in reaching a common understanding. And yet, persons altogether untrained in such work are given large discretion to decide what literature may be allowed to reach their fellow citizens without menace to their morals.

Most Americans undoubtedly believe that someone must have authority to keep obscene matters out of the mails. Bertrand Russell has, on occasion, argued that the removal of all restraint on such literature would be the best policy and one which, after a short initial upsurge in offensive matter, probably would actually diminish the total volume of obscene material. No doubt this is a risk that most citizens would not wish to take.

Since there probably is support for some such scrutiny of the mails, the object ought to be to safeguard the process against abuse, so far as possible. The best safeguard, it would appear, is the same sort of safeguard upon which we have insisted for those accused of other crimes. This is, of course, the trial by due process of the persons accused of violating the law. Let those accused of putting into the mails matter they cannot legally carry be arrested, charged, indicted, tried, and convicted or acquitted, and sentenced or freed, just as other persons accused of crimes are dealt with in the courts.

The post-office officials, of course, argue that this would allow the objectionable publications to move through the mails, and they argue that it is not feasible, on that account, to give those accused of mailing obscene matter even a hearing.

The Court of Appeals for the District of Columbia gave this argument short shrift in Walker *v.* Popenoe.[6] It said:

We are not impressed with the argument that a rule requiring a hearing before mailing privileges are suspended would permit, while the hearing was going on, the distribution of publications intentionally obscene in plain defiance of every reasonable standard. In such a case the effective remedy is the immediate arrest of the offender for the crime penalized by this statute. Such action would prevent any form of distribution of the obscene material by mail or otherwise. If the offender were released on bail the conditions of that bail should be a sufficient protection against repetition of the offense before trial. But often mailing privileges are revoked in cases where the prosecuting officers are not sure enough to risk criminal prosecution. That was the situation here. Appellees have been prevented for a long period of time from mailing a publication which we now find contains nothing offensive to current standards of public decency. A full hearing is the minimum protection required by due process to prevent that kind of injury.

Notwithstanding this opinion, the Department has continued to seize mail conceived by its officials to be obscene.

For a great many years, the Department followed a practice that had every appearance of the kind of prior restraint plainly offensive to the First Amendment. Publishers sent their texts to the Solicitors General of the Department, in advance of mailing, and the Department then advised the publishers if the books or magazines thus submitted were mailable. Postmaster General Frank C. Walker regarded this as censorship and abolished the censorship board and notified publishers that this would not be done any more.

In October 1955, something very like this practice again seemed to be in effect. In August, the postmaster at Mount Morris, Illinois, notified the magazine *Confidential*, which was printed there, that on orders from Washington no more copies were to be mailed until the legal office of the Post Office Department had reviewed sample copies and passed judgment on their 'mailability.'

The magazine took the matter into United States District Court in the District of Columbia. Judge Luther W. Youngdahl threw out the Post Office Department's temporary order holding up the mailing of the criticized issue of the magazine. In the last week in October 1955, the Post Office Department announced that it was clearing the January issue after examining advance copies and finding nothing unmailable in them.

Sensational magazines of this kind no doubt are offensive to a great many people. It is difficult to see how they can be reached by such methods, however, without putting in jeopardy the right of citizens generally to use the mails. The safest method, and in the long run the best method, surely would be to proceed as the government proceeds against others accused of crime, by ordinary due process. The penalties for wrongful mailing are severe enough to exert a wholesome restraining influence if their enforcement were sought in the courts.

### State and Local Restraints

States and localities, in recent years, have attempted more and more restrictions on the distribution of printed matter, largely as the result of widespread opposition to the dissemination of publications that citizens have believed have contributed to juvenile delinquency or that have advocated subversive doctrines.

Pressures from civic and religious groups caused thirty of the forty-six legislatures which met in 1955 to consider bills broadening the definition of obscenity to cover crime and horror comics, in some instances magazines and paper-bound books as well, and prohibiting display or sale of certain types of publications to minors.

Some of these bills were so extreme that, literally applied, they would have stopped the sale of the Bible.

Out of this welter of legislation emerged one possible answer. A group of Minnesota librarians sought some means of satisfying the clamor for better control of obscene literature that would not put freedom of expression in jeopardy.[7] They supported a bill drawn up by Professor Robert McClure of the Minnesota Law School. This bill provided: (1) prompt action (by interlocutory order) prohibiting the general sale of any obviously pornographic or obscene publication; (2) a district court action to adjudicate the alleged obscenity, with an open hearing and a written opinion by the responsible judge; (3) protection to dealers, druggists, and newsstand operators against censorship through coercion, or possible criminal indictment, by bringing action against the publication instead of the retailer (the dealer can then know with assurance what he may or may not sell); and (4) responsible judgment on matters of obscenity by jurists experienced in the evaluation of evidence instead of amateurs, volunteer 'censors,' or local law enforcement officials not specifically trained in such matters.

Neither this bill, nor a more sweeping bill for book and magazine censorship, passed. The Minnesota librarians may have pointed the way to a solution of some of these problems. Their measure would have the virtue of settling in the courts issues that are being handled by much more reckless methods.

Many local ordinances, imitating some of the state measures, have also emerged in recent months. The City Council of Jackson, Mississippi, for example, passed an ordinance outlawing the sale of publications 'conducive to crime' delinquency and general disorder.'

The difficulty with such measures, of course, lies in determining what publications are objectionable and by whose standards the determination is to be made.

## Police Interference with Distribution

New forms of police interference with distribution of printed material have developed in the past few years.

A much-imitated method is that of the Detroit police department, which simply warns dealers that it thinks certain titles violate obscenity laws. The distributors usually cooperate by withholding the books and the list of books they have withheld have been made the basis of similar action elsewhere.

The *Detroit News,* in an article published 5 May 1955 and reprinted in part in the Bulletin of the American Book Publishers Council of July 1955, disclosed that the processes by which the police determine that a book is objectionable are questionable to say the least. The *News* quoted the assistant prosecutor, John J. Rusineck, whose opinion forms the basis of warnings to distributors, on the test he uses. He said he advised distributors that it would be a violation of the law to distribute a book 'if I feel that I wouldn't want my 13-year-old daughter reading it.'

The Detroit pocket books methods are to be tested by the Michigan Supreme Court. It is difficult to bring such police control to a test in many jurisdictions. If dealers are cowed and intimidated, there is no easy way for citizens to reach the action of the police through the courts.

### Private Censorship

In many parts of the country strictly private groups have organized themselves into unofficial censors, issuing credentials to dealers who surrender their rights to control their own purchases and withholding them from dealers who refuse to knuckle under. In some cases, boycotts coerce dealers into compliance. These self-appointed censors, in many ways, are as dangerous as official agents. With no authority but their own, they assert the right to tell whole communities what they may and may not read. Today's interference with the distribution of publications they find obscene may easily be followed by tomorrow's interference with the distribution of material they find politically objectionable.

No democratic community can safely put into the hands of such a volunteer posse the right of citizens to read what they choose. The threats, intimidation, and boycotts utilized by some of these self-appointed committees constitute an indefensible kind of mob justice through which booksellers and newsdealers have been deprived of property rights. Public opinion would not tolerate this kind of lynch law invoked against the meanest felons. Selling offensive publications may be a bad thing. It is no worse thing than murder, arson, rape, and assault, and no law-abiding community would allow mob justice to impose its own punishment for these offenses. The high moral purpose of the citizens who attempt to enforce on others their own literary standards does not clothe such coercive practices with respectability.

This is not to say that the 'filthy picture' dealers ought to be allowed to conduct their business in violation of the law. The penalties for obscenity are severe. They ought to be enforced; but they ought to be enforced by duly constituted authority under which accused persons enjoy their constitutional rights to defend themselves and their property.

## Dangers of Censorship

The threats to morality and decency presented by obscene literature are obvious, self-evident, and conspicuous. The threats to freedom and democracy inherent in censorship are not so easily demonstrated. Some of these dangers have been pointed out by Edward de Grazia in a study published in 1955 by Duke University. He writes:

What the American public has not yet recognized is that, by sanctioning governmental censorship, it permits neurotic minds to project their collective neurosis and their sexual mores onto all of American literature and art. Further, it lends its weight to the morally insidious and politically dangerous proposition that the average American man is, and is expected by his government to be, psychologically incapable of controlling his own impulses or sorting out his own thoughts. Whenever a piece of literature or art, of whatever kind, is seized and condemned by the Post Office Department, Americans are advised by their own government that their minds and their souls are too weak to withstand, accept or reject such thoughts as are presented; that they require their government to save them from inner dissolution, corruption and depravity.[8]

## Other Interferences

Distribution of publications frequently has been fatally interfered with in recent years by breakdowns of the elaborate organization of truckers, dealers, distributors, agents, and carriers upon which citizens depend for their printed material.

Philadelphia newspaper readers were prevented from exercising their right to read the *Inquirer*, the *Record* and the *Evening Bulletin* for fifteen days in 1946 when Philadelphia Newspaper and Magazine Chauffeurs and Handlers went on strike.

We have grown so accustomed to these interruptions of the normal delivery of merchandise and services that most citizens probably make no distinction between one sort of inconvenience and another. Yet, in this case, that of which citizens were deprived was not just a passing convenience. The strike withheld from the whole community all the information for which it ordinarily relied upon newspapers. These publications were not destroyed, to be sure, but readers who did not and could not read their newspapers suffered losses of great seriousness in terms of the operation of a democratic society. It was quite immaterial — to the reader — that the newspapers continued to have the right to get news, the right to print it without prior restraint, the right to print without fear of punishment, and the right of access to publication materials. Deprivation of all the benefits of a free press contemplated by the Constitution could not have been more complete for those who could not get papers, if all these rights had been abolished by governmental decree.

Similar deprivation of right was enforced on readers in New York City in 1946. What the laws had assured readers in theory was for weeks denied them in practice.

The 1951 action of the Buenos Aires Union of News Vendors against *La Prensa* is, of course, the classic example of the strangulation of freedom of the press by a breakdown in distribution.

On 25 January, the union delivered an ultimatum to the newspaper, demanding that it eliminate all branch offices, acknowledge the union as the sole distribution device, and pay a commission of 20 per cent on all classified advertisements. The striking union prevented distribution of the paper, and when its publication was attempted on 27 February, workers were fired upon. The property then was seized by the government and retained until December 1955.

Comparison of what happened to *La Prensa* with what happened in New York and Philadelphia may seem strange, at first blush. And yet, these obstructions really differ only in the length of time involved, so far as the basic rights of readers are concerned. Of course, the role of government differed enormously. In the American cases, government, at worst, failed to prevent private persons from interfering with distribution. In the Argentina case, government countenanced if it did not inspire the obstruction of distribution. In all three cases, the people suffered a loss of their right to know.

What safeguard can be erected against the enforcement of 'secrecy' in this manner?

It is difficult to see a remedy that might not be worse than the evil. The only visible alternative to the conventional settlement of labor disputes would be some kind of governmental restraint upon the operations of unions engaged in these enterprises. And if the unions were to be restrained, it would be remarkable if some kind of government control did not also descend upon the publishing institutions. The risk of private interference with distribution would then have been met only by invoking the risk of governmental interference with the whole publication enterprise.

Such interpositions as these must be seen for what nonetheless they are. They are a serious threat to public channels of communication. They can set at naught all the elaborate precautions to preserve the right to know against governmental interference.

### Voluntary Newsdealer Action

The voluntary actions of news-distributing establishments may also put the last phase of public communications out of business.

In 1950, the Newsdealers Association of Greater New York

voted four to one to ban the *Daily Worker* from its five hundred newsstands. On another occasion it had exhibited its hostility to a Nazi publication. *Editor and Publisher*, commenting on the action against the *Worker*, clearly saw the risks involved here. It said:

. . . it's wrong for them to set themselves up as a censorship over what the public may buy. . . It is not inconceivable that this association of newsdealers may some day harbor a gripe against the New York Journal–American, or the Post, or the Times. . . Suppose the railway clerks refused to handle the Saturday Evening Post? Suppose the mail refused to work for the Herald Tribune?

The risks involved in constituting newsdealers censors need no further elaboration. Whether they act on their own motion, indulging their own prejudices and resentments, or respond to the prejudices and resentments of customers, the newsdealers are no safer custodians of the public's right to read than any other private group. If they can combine to freeze a Communist publication off the news racks today, they can combine to freeze a Republican newspaper off the racks tomorrow. Either action is an insupportable interference with the right of citizens to read.

The right to distribute, essential as it is to the whole process of printing and dissemination that lies between writer and reader, is by no means secure. Few citizens even regard it as a right indispensable to their enjoyment of the freedom of the press. Even if they so recognize it, the means of asserting the right are not established in statutes, courts, or customs. Where the right has suffered in this country, the protests often have been barely discernible. Yet, without it, the freedom to print is no more than the freedom to pile up soiled newsprint in warehouses. The last link in the chain of rights that make up the right to know surely is among the weakest. Americans may have to strengthen it in some fashion or see the First Amendment diminished, from time to time, into a fine theory without practical effect.

# 10

---

## The Channel Of The Public Papers

*The way to prevent these irregular interpositions of the people is to give them full information of their affairs through the channel of the public papers, and to contrive that those papers should penetrate the whole mass of the people. The basis of our government being the opinion of the people, the very first object should be to keep that right; and were it left to me to decide whether we should have a government without newspapers, or newspapers without a government, I should not hesitate a moment to prefer the latter.* — THOMAS JEFFERSON *

A PEOPLE whose government interposed no restraints upon the freedom of any medium of information still might be informed inadequately upon the transactions of its public agencies and about the life around it.

Upon many public issues a secrecy might be enforced that would be quite as effective, and quite as damaging to democratic principles, as if it were enforced by the government itself.

* *The Papers of Thomas Jefferson*, Julian Boyd (ed.), Princeton University Press, Princeton, 1955, vol. XI, p. 49.

This state of affairs might result from the inadequacy and ineffectiveness, or from the pollution and corruption, of the private institutions depended upon to make practical use of the freedom which constitutions and laws contemplate in theory.

Our system of government does not make the informing of the people inevitable or automatic; it only makes it possible for private agencies to achieve that objective. Governments make it possible for their citizens to be informed to the extent that they desist from prior restraint, from irregular punishment for wrongful publication, from secrecy in public affairs, from obstruction of access to printing facilities, or from interventions in the distribution of publications.

The private means for realizing these goals never have been perfect, in the United States or in any other country. They have been very imperfect indeed at intervals in this country's history.

Probably there never has been a more hopeful estimate of the press than that which appears at the head of this chapter, in a paragraph taken from Thomas Jefferson's famous letter to Edward Carrington, written on 16 July 1787. Yet, on 11 June 1807, in a letter to John Norvell, Jefferson appraised the American press in terms seldom exceeded for their severity. He said:

It is a melancholy truth, that a suppression of the press could not more completely deprive the nation of its benefits, than is done by its abandoned prostitution to falsehood. Nothing can now be believed which is seen in a newspaper. Truth itself becomes suspicious by being put into that polluted vehicle. The real extent of this state of misinformation is known only to those who are in situations to confront facts within their knowledge with the lies of the day . . . that man who never looks into a newspaper is better informed than he who reads them; inasmuch as he who knows nothing is nearer to truth than he whose mind is filled with falsehoods and errors.[1]

Foreign visitors in the early decades of the nineteenth century had a low opinion of American newspapers, too. Alexis

de Tocqueville already has been quoted on the coarseness of
the American press at the time of his visit, just prior to 1835.
In another comment he said:

In America three quarters of the enormous sheet are filled with advertisements, and the remainder is frequently occupied by political
intelligence or trivial anecdotes; it is only from time to time that one
finds a corner devoted to passionate discussions like those which the
journalists of France every day give to their readers.[2]

Frequently, Americans critical of today's press like to hark
back to press giants of the latter decades of the last century.
William Allen White has painted an unforgettable picture of
the typical country editor of the middle 'eighties:

He was too often, for all his pomp and bluster, the creature of his
banker. The editor borrowed with a prodigal hand, built a grand
house in the fashionable part of town; and, having passes, he rode up
and down the earth, a dashing figure, and mingled with the rich and
great in politics. But too frequently the editor was a pasteboard hero,
who when the times changed and factional fighting ceased in America, caved in and went to the scrap heap — a disheveled, vain, dis-
credited old pretender.[3]

Many more such criticisms of the American press, prior to
this century, might be cited to show that the medium of information which the First Amendment was designed to shelter
often has been held in very low esteem. The newspapers, in fact,
have been under continuous attack for coarseness, bad taste, dis-
honesty, error, falsehood, and mischief of almost every kind.
They have often deserved it. This does not prove that
criticisms of the contemporary press ought to be taken lightly.
It does seem to indicate that the virtues inherent in the freedom
of the press somehow continue to confer their benefits upon
democratic society even when the instruments through which
this freedom makes itself felt are themselves far from perfect.

This is a period of searching examination of the press. It is
a time of widespread and vigorous criticism of the press. And
it is a good thing. Those who honestly believe that it is unsafe to set up any custodian of press freedoms more exclusive

than the whole people will want the people to criticize the press with the greatest freedom and force. It never will be so good that it cannot be made better. At the same time, it is well to remember, it has been pretty bad in the past without failing in the essential purpose entrusted to it by those who fashioned the First Amendment. Their purposes, fortunately, did not require a press that was perfect. They had no experience with a perfect press in their own time. Their faith was in a press that was far, far from perfect as a means of information.

We have need for a much better press than eighteenth-century democratic institutions required. A hundred changes have worked to make the opinion of the masses of the people more influential in the formation of governmental policy. And numberless changes have operated to make the actions of government more controlling in the destiny of individual citizens. Citizens have, therefore, more power to influence governmental policy, and government action has more bearing on each American. So we need a press better than that which we had in the eighteenth or nineteenth centuries.

Generalizations about the press, however, ought to be made most cautiously. About the only safe generalization about the 'press' is that, for the most part, it operates by putting bits of graphite on pieces of white paper, by one process or another. Even this generalization no longer is accurate. There are daily newspapers with circulations as little as twenty-five hundred readers; and some with circulations as great as four million readers. Some have incomes as small as thirty-five thousand dollars a year; and some have incomes of more than thirty million dollars a year. Some newspaper plants are worth as little as fifty thousand dollars; some as much as one hundred million dollars. Some are privately owned. Some are owned by partnerships. Some are owned by corporations. Some are owned by churches and philanthropic institutions. Some are owned by their employees. Some are owned by labor unions.

Some are individually owned. One third are owned by groups or chains.

There is great variation even among the daily newspapers of general circulation, and when the whole 'press' (including all media of information) is comprehended within the meaning of the word, the variety is infinitely greater. Meaningful criticism, therefore, must be directed at the individual institutions.

Still, there are many expressions of vague dissatisfaction with the press as a whole. Many Americans seem to feel that, with all the opportunity it has to inform, to combat ignorance and secrecy, it is not fulfilling the duties and responsibilities imposed upon it. The criticism of the daily newspaper, as the oldest and still the primary source of information, probably is most severe.

Perhaps a great deal of such criticism is inevitable. The daily newspapers, day after day, fail in what they attempt to do, because they attempt the impossible. They attempt to tell readers what is happening all over the world, why it is happening, and what ought to be done about it. They do not succeed. They come nearer to succeeding than any daily press ever has come, in any country, at any time; but they still fall far short of compressing into manageable space that the average citizen has time to read, all that is occurring in the world.

The average newspaper reader no doubt is reconciled to this sort of failure, springing from the utter inability of ordinary men to gather from the ends of the earth reports on all events as complete, as accurate, and as impartial as the reader could gather for himself. Prepared as he is, or should be, for such failures, he nevertheless judges each particular news report by this standard, whenever and wherever he can test his newspaper against his own firsthand observations.

Judged by this standard, the newspaper does not succeed. It is imperfect and it is imperfectible to this extent. Readers who make allowance for such shortcomings are not put off by this explanation. They do not think that newspapers are doing as well as they could be doing, making all allowance for the fact that the goals they seek are unattainable.

There are criticisms of today's press quite as severe as those made in earlier periods. Perhaps they are even more severe.

### Control by Advertisers

It has been estimated that daily newspapers get from 49 to 82 per cent of their income from advertisers. The suspicion frequently is voiced that forces upon which the newspapers are so largely dependent for income must greatly influence newspaper handling of news, features, and editorials.

This influence is not as large as critics believe. It is kept at a minimum by the diversity of interests among advertisers themselves, who are not by any means of the same opinion as to what newspapers ought to print or suppress. It is curtailed by the separation of news and advertising responsibilities, so complete in metropolitan newspapers that editors feel free to accept or reject suggestions of business departments. It is diminished by the strengthening, year by year, of the doctrine of separate interest, which more and more confines the advertiser's claim upon newspaper space to the columns for which he pays.

Advertiser influence is most formidable in communities where mores and customs give an exceptional unanimity to local opinion in the business community. While advertisers, in theory, purchase space because they expect it to sell merchandise for them, like other buyers they favor their friends when other things are equal.

This sort of favoritism is not likely to be of long duration or profound significance. Space buyers, from time to time, or for a short interval, may choose media for reasons other than their merits. The unsentimental commercial system takes care of those who do it habitually. The newspaper which is the most effective advertising medium (whatever its views) usually gains dominance in its local market by the steady operation of commercial laws. Those who advertise in it gain more and more patronage and success at the expense of those who bestow their advertising on the basis of friendship and favoritism. The prejudiced buyers abandon their prejudices or abandon their business and the preponderant commercial support ultimately moves toward a proper correspondence with the real effectiveness of the newspaper as an advertising medium.

It is possible to cite cities in which the failure of a newspaper with a distinctly minority point of view to gain advertising support has contributed to its suspension. The *Bangor Commercial,* of Bangor, Maine, failed to maintain itself as a Democratic newspaper in that city of preponderantly Republican business institutions; but it had not succeeded at any point in offering advertisers a greater practical value as a medium for advertising than the larger *Bangor News.* If it had gained circulation advantage, the advertising might have developed.

The opinions of the business community, however, are seldom so much in accord. And where they are united in hostility to the views of a very independent newspaper, it can still make its way with national and classified advertisers who do not share the local display advertiser's prejudices. In the normal commercial community from which the newspaper draws its support, some diversity of opinion can be counted upon.

The direct intervention of the individual advertisers in the handling of newspaper content is an even rarer phenomenon. From time to time, an advertiser will attempt to influence newspaper content by his special position as the client, patron, or customer of a newspaper. His power to do so is greatly diminished by the fact that in most cases he is much more dependent upon the newspaper than the newspaper is dependent upon him, and reporters and editors know it. The foundation of the newspaper, as an effective advertising medium, is the credibility which its contents command from its readers.

Few newspapers are so shortsighted as to yield to the obvious and open coercion of an advertiser in a manner certain to damage the newspaper as an institution. Honesty is recommended as a practical policy, with the added virtue of moral rectitude attached.

Most advertisers are content with the space inside the rule that surrounds their commercial pleas. In some categories of advertising there are vestigial remnants of the days when the advertiser's influence pervaded adjacent columns. Many newspapers still consent to keep airline accident stories off pages containing airline advertising. This is a mild sort of acquiescence to advertiser influence. It is of not much practical importance in the flow of the news, even if it does have the bad smell of a generally bygone day when accidents to advertisers did not happen on the pages of the country press.

Now and then, relatively large advertisers will withdraw commitments under circumstances that leave upon editors the impression that the act is not disassociated from something the newspaper said about the advertiser. This sort of 'punishment' is seldom persisted in very long, however, and it probably increases rather than diminishes the resistance of honorable newspapers to such pressures.

Advertisers certainly have very little influence on the broad policies of the respectable newspaper. Now and then, their position may give them entrée that can be used to get a mention of some commercial event directly connected with an advertiser's establishment. It is not demonstrable that the 'mention' is often gauged so as to be in proportion to the advertiser's patronage. The days when the 'big advertiser' argument could be used effectively on editors are gone, along with the 'big advertisers' who tried to use such methods, for the most part.

The National Commission on Freedom of the Press, which was very critical of newspapers in many other respects, did not find advertiser influence a serious threat to the public's access to information.

Perhaps support by advertisement is not an ideal method of maintaining media of public information. Yet, it surely can be demonstrated that it is a great deal better than many alternative methods. It certainly is better than the concealed subsidies of party organizations as a means of press support. It surely is a lot better than government subsidies which leave newspapers the prisoners of political power. It has proven to be more reliable financially than reader support, with which one publication after another has experimented and which even the *Reader's Digest* ultimately found unsatisfactory as a sole source of revenue.

## Business Domination

It is pretty easy to show any fair critic that newspapers are not dominated by advertisers. It is not as easy to demonstrate their independence from the influence of the great commercial community of which they are a part.

One of the strongest statements of this case against the objectivity and impartiality of the press was made by the late Oswald Garrison Villard, who said:

Since no one would dream of starting a metropolitan newspaper with less than ten or even fifteen millions in the bank, the daily everywhere takes its place as an important industrial enterprise, a big business whose proprietors are entitled to rank among the foremost mercantile leaders of the community. Their tendency is naturally to think and act as do the members of the economic group to which they belong, and to drift steadily away from the plain people and especially from the workers. Just as the profession of journalism has changed into a business, so there is every temptation for the proprietor to consider all political and economic questions from the point of view of those who have large economic stakes and to look with alarm upon all proposed social and political reforms. The newspaper owner feels that he belongs in the Chamber of Commerce and the merchants' association more naturally, perhaps, than anybody else except the heads of the public utilities. His property ranks with those powerful business corporations which in every American community dominate its economic and financial life, whose officials and their wives set the 'society' tone and too often control social progress.[4]

This sounds like a reasonable piece of conjecture, at first examination; but there are some forces working against this premise that the typical newspaper identifies itself with the business community of which it is quite undeniably an important part.

The 'business community' is not the monolithic entity that Mr. Villard's criticism envisions. Within the commercial life of every city there is a great deal of division. A newspaper that tried to stand behind the business interests would find that the business interests do not stand still or stand in the same place. 'Business' may pursue its economic interest, but different businesses see their economic interests differently. The natural and obvious conflict between the domestic manufacturer and the importer on the tariff is only an example of the sort of differences that exist inside the business community.

There are like conflicts between producers of electricity and gas and the users of electricity and gas; between uptown business and downtown business; between New England textile manufacturers and South Atlantic textile manufacturers; between motion picture producers and television networks; between truckline operators and railroad corporations; between creditors and debtors.

There is no monolithic business community the members of which think alike and act alike on all great national issues. To use Mr. Villard's words, 'the members of the economic group' to which newspaper publishers belong do not think alike and act alike.

Even on many general issues there is always a great deal of dissent from the pronouncements of the National Association of Manufacturers and the United States Chamber of Commerce. The newspaper owner who wished to think and act like the members of his economic group would have to choose between the NAM, the Chamber of Commerce, the Committee on Economic Development, and the National Planning Association on a great many issues.

The alienation of businessmen from 'the plain people' and 'the workers' is not a universal rule as the Villard theory presupposes, either. The classic example of this sort of deviation, of course, was Joseph Fels, who in 1907 loaned the Russian Social Democratic Labour Party Congress which met in London seventeen hundred pounds sterling without interest. The press would have had a hard time agreeing with this particular businessman without agreeing also with some of the plainest of the 'plain people,' including most of the leaders of the Russian Revolution of 1917. Fels cannot be dismissed as unique in the annals of American business. The stereotype-word 'business' covers a great many points of view, ranging from political left to political right.

Probably it can be argued that on many national issues *most* business interests are on one side. Even if all newspapers felt a sense of identity with the side taken by 'most' business, the situation would not be quite as simple as the proposition posed by Mr. Villard, with its inference of united business attitudes on the great issues that divide the country.

The Villard theory is further weakened by the stubborn refusal of a great many large publishing enterprises to feel a sense of identity with the point of view supported by 'most' business. The conservative business elements (and this is what Mr. Villard probably meant by his paragraph) would like to be as sure as Villard was sure that they could count on a sense of identity in the press. The list of newspapers which do not exhibit any evidence that they regard themselves as a part of the conservative business community is long enough to make these newspapers far more than exceptions that prove the rule. The *New York Daily News*, for many years, was hardly a champion of the business point of view. The *New York Post*, now owned by Dorothy Schiff of the very wealthy Schiff family, has not been a mouthpiece for business. The *Chicago Sun-Times*, owned by the Marshall Field interests, exhibits no tendency to 'think' or 'act' with the members of the economic group to which it belongs. The *Louisville*

*Courier-Journal* and the *Louisville Times* must pain the NAM more than they please it. These are very large business enterprises indeed, but, like hundreds of other newspapers, they fail to identify themselves with any economic group in the communities where they are published, or in the nation.

Publishers, like the rest of us, no doubt are influenced largely by environment. Their responsibilities for the financial and commercial interests of newspaper properties obviously throw them into business and social contact with persons of large property interests. No doubt they are influenced by these contacts. Their fellow club men and golfing companions, however, do not all think alike. And even if they did, publishers are not sheltered from differing points of view. The editors and reporters who work on newspapers also come into contact with newspaper publishers and owners. They have the power and authority, in many instances, to order, to command, and to direct policy. A newspaper is a little different from a box factory, however, and newspaper policies are seldom enforced by the absolute command of an owner. The professional newspapermen who work for the owner or publisher are the product of experience and training which make their advice quite as influential on the publisher as that of his casual acquaintances in the locker room. Owners and publishers, moreover, are dependent upon their employees for implementation of policy by the thousands of decisions that are required to put the newspaper together each day. If the publisher feels an identity with persons of property, as Mr. Villard says he does, the editors and reporters are just as likely to feel that they have an identity with Mr. Villard's 'plain people' and 'workers.'

Publisher and editors and reporters, moreover, however much they may be divided in fundamental beliefs on political and economic issues, are likely to be united in the belief that the success of the newspaper, in the end, depends upon the credibility with which it is read by readers. That credibility, in turn, depends upon a more impartial attitude than that into which Mr. Villard, and like critics, fear the press is likely to be led by the climate in which newspaper owners live and move.

Newspapers, to a far greater degree than Mr. Villard and other like-minded critics might suppose, do regard themselves as members of a 'Fourth Estate' which, however much it may sympathize with one group or another, acknowledges the need to maintain a degree of independence.

If the press is not identified with any one segment of the national life to the point of partiality toward it, it must be acknowledged that a press resting upon the broad base of readers and enterprise inside a country is going to be biased in favor of the country, as it sees its interests. It may exhibit, from time to time, plenty of hostility toward an administration of the government, but it is hardly likely to exhibit hostility toward the very form of the government in the support of which the overwhelming numbers of all its supporters are united. It is likely to be characterized by loyalty to the country's institutions. So long as these cherished institutions include the right to dissent, to criticize, to disagree, this loyalty is not likely to be dangerous to the principles embodied in the First Amendment.

The press, in this, tends to reflect opinion as well as to make it. Perhaps it may be predisposed to support the status quo. In a period in which revolutionary change is necessary, this might be some disadvantage. It would be even more dangerous to have a press that felt no sense of identity with existing institutions at any time. The kind of press existing in the colonies at the time of the Revolution identified itself overwhelmingly with the forces seeking change. The kind of press now existing in the country might react differently. The risk probably is one the country will be content to run.

No society has much concerned itself with maintaining an environment favorable to its overthrow in readiness for the day when public support was no longer deserved. We cannot expect our society to do so, either. There probably will be a bias in favor of existing institutions in any press except that supported and subverted by external subsidy.

## The One-Party Press

Ever since the 1952 elections there has been a great deal of concern about the possible effects on public life of a 'one-party press' in America.

*Editor and Publisher* found, during the 1952 campaign, that Eisenhower was supported by 67.34 per cent of the daily newspapers with 80.24 per cent of the circulation, while Stevenson was supported by only 14.52 per cent of the newspapers with only 10.68 per cent of the daily circulation.

Republican presidential candidates were supported by most of the daily newspapers in the preceding five elections, and during this period the results were cited as evidence that the press was impotent to influence the outcome. Since 1952 the argument has been that it has had too much influence. If newspapers had enough influence to determine the outcome of presidential contests, the present political division of the press would be most alarming to those who would like to preserve a two-party system. If the Republican complexion of the daily newspapers governs news coverage, or measurably distorts news handling, the situation would be worrisome.

Some newspapers are frankly partisan in editorial and in news columns; but most of them profess to be impartial in news coverage. It has not been easy to find out if they were or were not impartial in the 1952 campaign.

The newspaper objectivity of a group of eight newspapers was studied by Malcolm W. Klein and Nathan Maccoby.[5] Their inquiry convinced them that the Democratic newspapers, on the whole, favored Democratic candidates in news headlines, display, and text while the Republican newspapers favored Republican candidates in news headlines, display, and text.

Robert Batlin studied the behavior of the three San Francisco newspapers [6] in 1896 and in 1952 and found that the papers in 1952 published more news and pictures about the editorially supported party, that the contents of the news published was more favorable to the supported party, that the reporters and political editors made more favorable and less unfavorable statements about the supported party. They also found the 'imbalance' less serious in 1952 than it was in 1896.

Charles E. Higbie measured the campaign coverage of fourteen Wisconsin newspapers (thirteen of which supported Eisenhower) and found that the two major parties received roughly equal mention in column inches of stories but that the top headline ratio was sixty-three for the Republicans to thirty-seven for the Democrats.[7]

There were several other regional surveys of the kind but none of them established good ground for saying whether or not the campaign reporting as a whole was biased.

A committee of the newspaper fraternity, Sigma Delta Chi, began to prepare in the fall of 1955 for a 1956 survey that might disclose the amount of bias in the daily press reporting of the 1956 presidential campaign. It dropped these plans when a survey showed most newspaper publishers and editors hostile to the project.

It is difficult to determine the fairness of a newspaper's political coverage. Someone has to decide first what is fair. You cannot start with the assumption that each political party and each candidate is entitled to exactly the same amount of coverage, the same position, and the same type display. In the early weeks of the 1952 campaign, Republican and Democratic newspapers alike, in one study, gave more space and bigger headlines to Eisenhower simply because he was better known at this stage of the contest. There is a great deal of variation in the skill with which presidential campaigns are waged. Not only the newsmaking gifts of the candidates but the skill and efficiency of their press organizations, as well, are involved.

If one candidate makes effective, newsworthy speeches, always has advance texts promptly available, and if his press officers make it possible for reporters to reach telegraph facilities, obtain access to meetings, get answers to questions, arrange their own itineraries in advance, and otherwise operate effectively, that candidate is likely to be well covered, whatever the views of editors.

If another candidate says little that is new or original, if his texts are never available in advance, if reporters are stranded away from telephones and telegraph lines, if newsmen cannot get access to meetings, if they cannot get answers to questions, if the campaign plans are uncertain and subject to abrupt changes, if stories about the candidate habitually reach newspaper offices after press start time — that candidate is likely to fare none too well in the news, whatever the editorial support he may have.

In a way this is unfortunate, but perhaps at the same time the relative efficiency with which campaigns are managed may constitute some kind of a rough index of the administrative ability of the candidates.

The audience of a given newspaper is also a factor in its campaign coverage. A daily newspaper published in a Southern city where 90 per cent of the readers are interested in the Democratic campaign and 90 per cent of the locally originating speeches are for the Democratic candidate probably will reflect to some degree its environmental bias. Similarly a newspaper in a state that always has gone Republican will reflect to some extent the bias of its readers. In both cases, the dominant party will actually make more news than the minority party.

Much of the news that influences voters would not be counted as political news at all. Battle reports in wartime may influence a campaign result more than speeches. Stories about falling farm prices or increasing unemployment may have more effect than campaign oratory.

Notwithstanding these difficulties, it should be possible by careful content analysis coupled with full appraisal to establish to the satisfaction of objective students whether or not an individual newspaper handles a given election campaign adequately. It should be possible to discover if its day-in and day-out coverage has been such as to convey to readers a fair estimate of the basis of each party's bid for support.

The matter of each newspaper's impartiality is not a subject of the same concern in countries where each newspaper is a party organ of avowed bias. It is a matter of particular concern where a single newspaper may be the source of the readers' information about the campaign. Readers do not have a right to ask that each candidate be given the same number of columns and the same number of headlines; but they have a right to ask that news editors make decisions on these matters with an open mind.

## The Negative Press

Bad news is too often good news to American newspaper editors, many newspaper critics complain. They protest that modern life is not all violence, disaster, murder, robbery, rape, arson, and sudden death.

The reader, of course, has two concerns about the amount of such news. He is rightly concerned about the sort of picture of the world that is conveyed to him and the rest of the public. And he is properly concerned with the degree to which sensational news of this kind usurps the available newspaper space and curtails the number of columns available for more serious and positive news.

Newspapermen themselves often have criticized the amount of crime news, and the manner of its presentation.

The historian of the *Manchester Guardian* once said of the owner of that newspaper:

To exploit popular ignorance, to play up the vices or weaknesses of half-formed characters and half-filled minds would have seemed to C. P. Scott no more worth considering than a policy of living on the profits of disorderly houses.

Horace Greeley, in criticizing the crime news of a sensational competing newspaper, said:

We weigh well our words when we say that the moral guilt in-
curred and the violent hurt inflicted upon social order by those
who thus spread out the loathsome details of the most damning deed,
are tenfold greater than those of the miscreant himself. . . The
wretched plea of the 'duty of the press to society' — that it is bound
to keep the public informed — is urged, but the same hypocrites
who stab the public good under this protection turn a deaf ear to
the higher duties which they owe to the good of their fellow-men
and to the requirements of decent morality.[8]

In August 1948, M. Louvel, a member of the French Chamber of Deputies, sought to diminish crime reporting in France.
He introduced a bill under which all crime would appear under
a single column head entitled, 'miscellaneous.' No individual
report was to have a headline. No more than twenty lines
were to be devoted to any one crime. No crime photographs
were to be permitted. The bill, of course, did not pass. Others
have thought crime news ought to be limited in some way,
however.

Yet, crime news serves some socially constructive purposes.
Its prevailing message to readers is that crime does not pay.
It assists law enforcement officials in the apprehension of criminals. It furnishes to the restraints of law the further restraint
on wrongful behavior represented by the fear of adverse publicity. It protects the public against the malfunctioning of law
enforcement agencies. These gains are not all offset by the
risk that it may inspire imitation, by the anguish it causes
criminals and friends of accused persons, by the degree to
which it may interfere with reform, or by the extent to which
it may sometimes offend good taste.

The good that results does not depend on the good motive
of publishers or editors. The purpose may be commercial, but
the results nonetheless constructive. The possible injury to society can be mitigated in great degree by the way the news
is handled — by shunning techniques that glorify crime, ro-
manticize criminals, or teach criminal methods. Responsible
papers try to do this.

A survey made in 1955 suggests that so-called negative news

may not dominate the newspapers to quite the degree that critics have supposed.[9]

This survey classified as 'negative' news dealing with international tension, conflict between nations, civic disruption, conflict between groups, crime and vice, accidents and disaster. Such news, it found, occupied 33.2 per cent of the Associated Press daily file and 33.5 per cent of the United Press daily file from 16 to 22 February 1953. Thirty-four newspapers using the wire services were studied and only one of the thirty-four made more use of the negative items on the file, proportionately, than of the positive items.

It must be acknowledged, however, that newspaper predilection for bad news rests, in part, upon the normal human being's attitude toward bad news. The first moments of a meeting between long-separated friends are most likely to be spent discussing deaths, accidents, and misfortunes that have occurred to friends, family, and associates since last they met. There is a normal assumption that things have gone well, unless there are reports to the contrary. So reports of the things that have gone badly spring first to mind. The deviation from normal behavior has more inherent interest than conformity to it.

Newspapers share mankind's general preoccupation with the negative events of the day, with the bad news from all quarters. In the present state of civilization there may be foundation for the argument that good news, by becoming rare, has become more newsworthy. Whether for this or other reasons, there is some evidence that the trend, if there is one, now runs in the direction of less emphasis upon at least the crime category of bad news, and considerably more on the stories of human triumph, success, achievement, and glory.

Whatever the wish or inclination of newspaper editors, however, there is a melancholy likelihood that the newspapers will continue to purvey a great deal of negative news, if that is defined to include news of all sorts of violence, disturbance, disaster, and turbulence. The primary reason for this is neither the instincts of humankind nor the special perversity of editors, but the perversity of life itself. It is really this perversity against which readers are in rebellion, and not the mere report of it. Readers long for the quiet and ease which they believe attended a more peaceful, tranquil period of human history.

It is too bad they cannot have it, but, unhappily, we must acknowledge the merit of a remark attributed to Lenin: 'The man who desires tranquillity should not have been born into the Twentieth Century.' Those who long for it probably will continue to complain about newspapers, the columns of which show clearly enough the lack of it. Like the ancient Greeks whose custom it was to destroy the bearers of bad tidings, they will continue to rail against the newspapers who bring them news they would not wish to read.

### Triviality in the Press

The great amount of trivial matter in American newspapers has been an object of criticism by foreign visitors and Americans ever since Tocqueville voiced this objection to the country's press in 1835.

The 'trivia' is objected to, of course, not just because it is of little merit itself, but because the large amount of it diminishes the space devoted to more serious matter.

A representative division of space on the average metropolitan daily newspaper probably would be an allocation giving the major departments about this percentage of nonadvertising space: general news 30 to 40 per cent; sports 15 per cent; financial news 7 per cent; women's affairs 10 per cent; comic strips 14 per cent; entertainment and information features 20 per cent; opinion and editorial comment 5 per cent. This of course varies from newspaper to newspaper, but I think might be regarded as typical of papers in cities of under two million population. About half the content of the paper is dedicated to amusement and entertainment material, in the form of features or reports on sports and recreational activities.

Much of the matter in the news columns occupying the other half of the newspaper probably would have to be described as 'trivia' also, in the sense that it is news about things that serious-minded people would regard as 'unimportant.'

Why the high percentage of nonnews content? Is this a matter of serious reproach? The average editor probably would not sweat long over a defense of this content. Most of it has reached the columns of his newspaper in response to the expressed (or estimated) demands of readers and in reaction to competition for the leisure time of citizens — a competition with other newspapers where they exist and with other media where there is no newspaper competition. It has been built up over a great many years. Much of it, no doubt, ought to be re-examined more frequently to see if the estimates of reader interest are not out of date.

The distribution of news and opinion is the first responsibility of the newspaper and the total appearance of some newspapers gives the impression that this first responsibility is being subordinated. One good result of the concentration of American newspapers on so-called 'trivia' ought to be noticed by their somewhat solemn critics, however, and that is the effect of entertainment content on the general distribution of newspapers. Jefferson's wish that the newspapers should 'penetrate the whole mass of the people' in order to justify the purpose of the press has been fulfilled. And that 'penetration' is owing in no small part to the entertainment and amusement content of the newspapers through which readership has been sustained and expanded. The comic strips, panels, and lovelorn columns have opened doors as advance agents for the more serious content of the press. The press of many other countries, adhering to older and more staid formulae, never have achieved the mass circulation characteristic of newspapers in the United States. It has been observed that the party press of pre-Nazi Germany never had the great dispersal, the enormous mass audience of our general circulation press, and Nazi attacks upon many excellent newspapers left the masses of the people unmoved. The 'light' content of the daily newspapers not only has broadened the base of newspaper circulation, but it has exposed to serious news and comment segments of the population that never would have purchased the sort of solemn journals which some critics think newspapers should become.

Personal taxicab surveys are not very scientific but they do furnish some sort of insight into a reader audience not otherwise often surveyed. In a great many interviews of this kind, it has been easy to discover that favorite comic strips lead many customers into the newspaper. By coupling this sort of inquiry with an inquiry into the 'most interesting' thing in the paper of a given date, some surprising information can be gained. A man who bought the newspaper to read 'Dick Tracy,' for example, unhesitatingly said he thought the news report on the Geneva conference the most interesting thing in the paper that day.

The American reader-audience probably is the most homogeneous in the world. Its tastes no doubt are more uniform than those of many other national reader groups. Even within this audience, however, there are great differences of education and interest. The sort of specialized newspapers that might please some reader groups more than the trivia-laden daily press would have some serious social disadvantages. It would make the better-informed more informed and the least-informed less informed, in the long run. It is not to be inferred from this comment that the average editor has laid a deliberate trap for the unwary comic strip devotee in order to snare him into contemplation of important matters of news and opinion. Nothing that subtle or conspiratorial has been happening. Yet, the result may be something quite like that, in some cases. The 'trivia' can so monopolize a newspaper's content as to lower general taste, no doubt. It can also be so balanced as to elevate the interests and tastes of persons who otherwise could not be enticed into printed pages.

The complaint about the 'trivia' in the news columns themselves is another matter. This complaint arises from a failure to appreciate the nature of news and from an assumption that the only important news is that which concerns affairs of government, science, education, etc. The news about public affairs, of course, is of greatest importance. It influences the lawmaking and governing processes of cities, states, and nations. We ought not to despise news of another kind however. The news about the everyday, ordinary trials and triumphs of ordinary people is also important. It enforces the mores, customs, and conventions of society and it makes new mores, customs, and conventions. The reaction of readers to news of this sort, in imitation or revulsion, constitutes a lawmaking process of quite as much social significance and ultimate political importance as the lawmaking that takes place in council chambers, state legislatures, and in Congress.

Rebecca West has ably pointed out that the conscious political propaganda is the least effective feature of a newspaper. As she puts it:

It is the presentation of the facts that matter, the facts that put together are the face of the age: the rise in the price of coal, the new ballet, the woman found dead in a kimona on the golf links, the latest sermon of the Archbishop of York, the marriage of a Prime Minister's daughter. For if people do not have the face of the age set clear before them, they begin to imagine it; and fantasy, if it is not disciplined by the intellect and kept in faith with reality by the instinct of art, dwells among the wishes and fears of childhood, and so sees life either as simply answering any prayer or as endlessly emitting nightmare monsters from a womb-like cave.[10]

There are small, fine lines and blemishes and imperfections in 'the face of the age,' but it is a mistake to dismiss them as irrelevant trivia as do some whose approach to the news is more solemn than discerning.

## The Uniformity of the Press

American newspapers are all alike, some critics complain. Oswald Garrison Villard frequently criticized the dread uniformity and monotony of our newspapers.

It is quite true that modern methods of distributing news and features have produced like content in hundreds of news-papers and have left very few really unique newspapers wholly dependent for their entire content on the work of their own staff.

Several years ago I measured a small group of daily news-papers and concluded that about 36 per cent of their content was from outside sources — syndicates and wire services.

They were, to this extent, a great deal like each other and a great deal like other newspapers similarly supplied.

It is difficult to imagine a newspaper of sufficient resources to dispense entirely with the services of the major news agencies or 'wire services,' even if it could be demonstrated that this would be desirable. Some of them do get along with-out the feature content supplied by the syndicates. There are nearly two hundred firms engaged in the business of furnishing comic strips, panels, columns, fashion notes, and kindred matter to the daily press. What's wrong with this? It has been argued that it produces a monotonous similarity in papers; limits job opportunities and diminishes talent at the source; en-trenches monopoly by conferring advantage on the newspapers that hold contracts for features; encourages the use of a cheap substitute for more expensive local staff; and diminishes the space available for more serious matter.

At the same time, it has improved the quality of smaller newspapers which could not possibly command such talent, if each artist or writer had a single outlet. It has widened the market and increased the rewards of the best creative artists. It has made available better material than single newspapers could buy. It has put into the columns of monopoly newspapers dissenting points of view. It has contributed to the homogeneity of the American people. It has increased the distribution of newspapers.

Basically, the syndicate system is a sort of co-operative buy-ing project on an enormous scale, through which the collec-tive purchasing power of many newspapers is pooled.

By making syndicated feature material available at a reasonable price, the system probably has increased the percentage of newspaper space devoted to lighter material. (Some newspapers have been aptly criticized for being more syndicate than sinning.) If there is a fault here, it is a fault for which individual newspapers and editors have the remedy. The dangers of the syndicate system, whatever they are, are not inherent in the system or inescapable.

### Are Weaknesses Fatal to Press Purposes?

These and other criticisms of the press are relevant to the theme of this study to the extent that the weaknesses of the press, whatever they are, prevent it from carrying out the purposes for which it has been granted certain immunities and privileges.

Are they so serious that newspapers do not achieve the results which the founding fathers thought would flow from the First Amendment?

Where government makes information available, permits publication without prior restraint, refrains from reprisal for hostile publication, keeps the avenues to printing facilities open, and allows free distribution, does the press fail to take advantage of these liberties?

Are the shortcomings in this respect so serious that those in government are justified in withholding information because of the reasonable apprehension that the press will not correctly pass it on to readers? Are they so grave that, at this late date, Americans ought to consider prior restraints on publication to prevent abuses? Are they so bad that hitherto unused sorts of reprisal by Congress and the executive branch ought to be invoked? Are they so dismaying that presses and equipment ought to be licensed? Are they so disturbing that distribution ought to be enjoined?

The people do not seem to think so. Raymond Nixon, in 1954, published a study of public attitudes toward eight daily newspapers in five different cities.[11] He asked the question:

'In general, do you think the papers try to be fair by presenting all sides of the news to the public?' Of the readers questioned, overwhelming majorities answered 'Yes.' The per-
centages returning affirmative answers for the eight newspapers:
76, 85, 85, 84, 85, 60.6, 87.6, 78.2. Toward four newspapers
for which earlier figures were available, confidence had increased from 1949 to 1953.

Periodic surveys by individual newspapers and by some research agencies, conducted from time to time, show a similar
high confidence in the accuracy and integrity and fairness of
newspapers.

Newspapers and other media are not succeeding altogether
in their undertaking to inform citizens better. Readers themselves are well aware of many individual lapses and shortcomings. Newspapers need to improve if they are to meet the increasing responsibilities that are laid upon them. At the same
time, it seems pretty clear that there is nothing on the record that
would make the weakness of the newspapers justification for
the refusal or failure of government to carry out its obligations to further public information.

The professed fears that information furnished by government will be distorted by the press or misunderstood by the
people are fears that spring from a lack of faith in democratic
institutions and beliefs. No legitimate excuse for secrecy can
be based upon the shortcomings of the press or the lack of
understanding in the people.

It is astonishing that such doubts and misgivings about the
release of information should be heard now. It is amazing
that such grounds for secrecy should be argued in open debate
or discerned in the behavior of officials, in this day and age.
No one dared advance such views in the eighteenth century
when most of the population of the country was illiterate. A
general and optimistic confidence in the informed judgment
of citizens prevailed when the government was formed. There
is better reason for that optimism now. More Americans than
ever before have been educated in our schools, trained in

public life, familiarized with events abroad and generally
equipped to weigh intelligently all sorts of public issues. Faith
in their right judgment has been vindicated by unnumbered
thousands of right decisions on public questions. Nothing that
has happened in the past, here on this continent, justifies any
belief that the times require secret government by some informed elite of the few who alone are wise, understanding,
compassionate, and omniscient.

The democratic process is in danger in a country the office-
holders and public servants of which exhibit a contempt and
doubt as to the judgment and stability of the rank and file of
the people. If such contempt and doubt persists it will drive a
fatal wedge between the governing and the governed and
carry all our democratic institutions down to destruction.

The trend toward secrecy in government, inspired by such
fears and doubts about the safety with which information for
the people can be given to the press, is pushing us farther and
farther away from the concept of a free people that is the
master and not the servant of its government.

The improvement of all our media of communication must
be an object of concern for all serious-minded citizens. Our
'press,' including every device for transmitting information
and ideas, needs to be made more efficient. Its imperfections
are a subject that ought to engage the attention of all those
who wish to keep our institutions. In all those respects in which
it is imperfect, however, it will not be improved by withholding from it information about government which hitherto
has been made available to it. The cure for its gravest defects
is not less but more access to the proceedings of government.

Those who are appointed and those who are elected to office
can not honestly put forward, as an excuse for secrecy, the
difficulties and deficiencies of the press. Nor can they justly
assert the danger that their intentions will be misunderstood
because of either the venality or stupidity of the press or the
ignorance of the people.

These excuses, showing as they do a lack of confidence in

popular judgment and democratic methods of forming it are occasion for a just alarm for, as Marc Bloch has so wisely said: 'A democracy becomes hopelessly weak, and the general good suffers accordingly, if its higher officials are bred to despise it.' [12]

The information of the people is the foundation of our whole political system. Secrecy threatens that foundation, on whatever pretext or for whatever good reason it is invoked. Citizens must have the right to get information, the right to print it or otherwise publish it without prior restraint, the right to print without punishment for harmless publication, the right of access to materials of publication, and the right to distribute. When they do not have these rights they cannot choose their public officials wisely or judge their policies intelligently.

The political acts and judgments of citizens who are fully informed are their own political acts and judgments; the political acts and judgments of citizens who are only partly informed are the political acts and judgments of those who partly inform them.

A government that generally asserts the right to say which of its acts may be divulged and which must be concealed exercises a power that tends to tyranny whatever its outward form. It has the power to enforce acceptance of its policies by exaggerating their merits and distorting their disadvantages. It has the means of concealing its crimes and derelictions and exaggerating its virtues and its triumphs. It possesses a device for accomplishing that greatest of all corruptions — the corruption of the mind of the public itself. A people, so corrupted, is a people no longer free, whatever the form and structure of its governmental agencies. It is in this sense that we are confronted with a choice between secrecy and freedom.

# NOTES

## CHAPTER ONE

1. David Hume, *History of England*, Edinburgh, 1809, vol. VI, p. 267.
2. Thomas Babington Macaulay, *The History of England*, Macmillan & Company, London, 1913–15, vol. III, p. 543.
3. Frederick Seaton Siebert, *Freedom of the Press in England, 1476–1776*, University of Illinois Press, Urbana, 1952, p. 103.
4. Ibid.
5. William M. Clyde, *The Struggle for Freedom of the Press from Caxton to Cromwell*, Oxford University Press, London, 1934, p. 135.
6. Harold Herd, *The March of Journalism*, George Allen & Unwin, Ltd., London, 1952, p. 27.
7. Laurence Hanson, *Government and the Press 1695–1763*, Oxford University Press, London, 1936, p. 32.
8. William Hartpole Lecky, *A History of England in the Eighteenth Century*, Longmans, Green & Co., London, 1878, vol. II, p. 445.
9. Hanson, op. cit. p. 82.
10. Clyde Duniway, *Freedom of the Press in Massachusetts*, Longmans, Green & Co., London, 1906, p. 41.
11. *Annals of the Congress of the United States*, vol. I, p. 16.
12. Ibid. p. 917.
13. Harold L. Cross, *The People's Right To Know*, Columbia University Press, New York, 1953, p. 183.
14. Hansard, 29 October 1946, p. 540.
15. Woodrow Wilson, *The New Freedom*, Doubleday, Page & Co., New York, 1913, p. 125.
16. Ibid. p. 129.
17. Harold L. Ickes, *The Secret Diary of Harold L. Ickes*, Simon and Schuster, New York, 1953, p. 515.

18. *Congressional Quarterly*, 24 November 1954.
19. 'Secret Sessions,' *The National Municipal Review*, vol. XXXIII, no. 5, May 1944, p. 218.
20. William Maclay, *Journal of William Maclay*, D. Appleton & Co., New York, 1890, p. 400.
21. Wilson, op. cit. p. 131.

CHAPTER TWO

1. David Hume, *History of England*, Edinburgh, 1809, vol. I, p. 255.
2. Donald G. Morgan, *The First Dissenter*, University of South Carolina Press, Columbia, 1954, p. 54.
3. John Henry Wigmore, *Treatise on the Anglo-American System of Evidence in Trials at Common Law*, Little, Brown and Co., Boston, 1940, vol. VI, p. 1835.
4. Sir William Blackstone, *Commentaries on the Laws of England*, printed for W. Strahan, T. Cadell, and D. Prince, London, 1783, p. 373.
5. Jeremy Bentham, *Rationale of Judicial Evidence*, Hunt and Clarke, London, 1827, vol. IV, p. 317.
6. *Rationale of Judicial Evidence*, vol. II.
7. *Rationale of Judicial Evidence*, p. 343 (Bowring's edition, 1843).
8. Cross, op. cit. p. 164.
9. Walter Lister, 'Secrecy Continues,' *ASNE Bulletin*, March 1954, p. 6.
10. A. S. Cutler, 'Judicial Administration and the Common Man,' *Annals of the American Academy of Political and Social Science*, May 1953, p. 107.
11. U.S. v. Kobli, Third Circuit Court, 3 February 1949.
12. District of Columbia v. Williams, Municipal Court, D.C., Criminal Division, No. 102,480, Fennel J., April 1952.
13. Rex v. Justices of Bodmin, (1947) 1 K.B. 321,325, quoted by Justice Frankfurter in his concurring opinion in Joint Anti-Fascist Refugee Committee v. McGrath, 341 U.S. 123, 172 n. 19 (1951).
14. United Press v. Valente, Court of Appeals, State of New York, vol. 308 N.Y. Reports, p. 85.
15. Ibid. p. 81.
16. Ibid. p. 89.
17. New York Post v. Samuel S. Liebowitz.
18. Cleveland News, 12 April 1955, p. 1.
19. *Cleveland Plain Dealer*, 13 April 1955, p. 1.

20. Thomas M. Cooley, *Constitutional Limitations*, Little, Brown and Co., Boston, 1927, vol. I, p. 647.
21. Ibid. p. 931.
22. Ibid. p. 135.
23. People *v.* Hartman, 103 California 1, 242.
24. Cross, op. cit. p. 169.
25. Senate Subcommittee on Juvenile Crime, 83rd Congress, vol. I, p. 205.
26. Fred W. Woodson, 'Newspaper Publication of Names of Juvenile Offenders,' *Focus*, published by the National Probation and Parole Association, September 1954, p. 152.
27. Wigmore, *Treatise on the Anglo-American System of Evidence in Trials at Common Law*, op. cit. p. 340.
28. Senate Subcommittee on Juvenile Crime, 83rd Congress, vol. I, pp. 6, 30, 207, 282, 394, 408, 414.
29. Edwin M. Otterbourg, 'Fair Trial and Free Press,' *Journal of the American Judicature Society*, vol. 37, no. 3, p. 80.
30. A. T. Burch, ' "Trial by Newspaper" Is Often Exercise of a Public Duty to Yell "Stop Thief!," ' *The Quill*, October 1954, p. 16.
31. Judge Philbrick McCoy, 'The Judge and Courtroom Publicity,' *Journal of the American Judicature Society*, vol. 37, no. 6, p. 180.
32. Stuart H. Perry, 'Perry Endorses Matthews' Stand,' *ASNE Bulletin*, no. 372, 1 January 1955, p. 11.
33. William J. Knight, 'Free Press and Fair Trial, An Address to the American Judicature Society,' 26 May 1954, p. 7.
34. *Editor and Publisher*, 25 December 1954, p. 39.
35. *Editor and Publisher*, 15 January 1955, p. 42; 25 December 1954, p. 26.

## CHAPTER THREE

1. Maclay, op. cit. p. 262.
2. Henry S. Randall, *Life of Thomas Jefferson*, Derby & Jackson, New York, 1858, vol. III, p. 211.
3. Cross, op. cit. p. 218.
4. The Constitution of Sweden, Document II:4, Chapter 2, Article 1, p. 82.
5. Letter to Andrew Ellicott, 18 December 1800, *The Writings of Thomas Jefferson*, Thomas Jefferson Memorial Association, Washington, 1904-5, vol. XIX, p. 121.
6. Leonard D. White, *The Jeffersonians, A Study in Administrative History 1801-1829*, The Macmillan Company, New York, 1952, p. 405.

7. Ibid., p. 406.
8. Leonard D. White, *The Jacksonians, A Study in Administrative History 1829–1861*, The Macmillan Company, New York, 1954, p. 147.
9. Federal Personnel Manual, Chapter Z 1, Section 29.11 (a).
10. James E. Pollard, *The Presidents and the Press*, The Macmillan Company, New York, 1947, p. 30.
11. Ibid. p. 501.
12. Ibid. p. 631.
13. Ibid. p. 705.
14. Ibid. p. 715.
15. Replies from Federal Agencies to Questionnaire Submitted by The Special Subcommittee on Government Information of the Committee on Government Operations, 1 November 1955.

## Chapter Four

1. Hanson, op. cit. p. 86.
2. Clyde, op. cit. p. 86.
3. Duniway, op. cit. p. 105.
4. *The Writings of Thomas Jefferson*, Thomas Jefferson Memorial Association, Washington, 1904, vol. XIII, p. 264.
5. Herbert Luethy, *France Against Herself*, Frederick A. Praeger, New York, 1955, p. 92.
6. United States Navy Public Relations Manual, Section 0818, Paragraph 9.
7. Air Force Regulations 190–10a.
8. Lloyd V. Berkner, Address before the Seventh Annual Conference on the Administration of Research, University of California, Berkeley, 2 September 1953.
9. Arthur Smithies, *The Budgetary Process in the United States*, The McGraw Hill Book Company, New York, 1955, p. 277.
10. Zechariah Chafee, Jr., *Government and Mass Communications*, The University of Chicago Press, Chicago, 1947, vol. I, p. 14.
11. 'National Security and Our Individual Freedom,' A Statement on National Policy by The Research and Policy Committee of the Committee For Economic Development, December 1949.
12. John P. Roche, 'Security and the Press,' *Current History Magazine*, October 1955, p. 229.
13. Ibid. p. 235.

## Chapter Five

1. Harold Cross, 'The Right of Privacy,' *The Bulletin of the American Society of Newspaper Editors*, No. 366, 1 June 1954, p. 1.

2. Ibid.
3. Gautier *v.* Pro Football, Inc., 278 App. Div. (NY) 431, 1951.
4. Woodrow Wilson, op. cit.
5. Welfare and Pension Investigation Report, 84th Congress, 1st Session, filed by the Subcommittee on Welfare and Pension Funds of the Senate Committee on Labor and Public Welfare, in response to Senate Resolution 225, p. 45.
6. Walter Lippmann, *The Public Philosophy*, Atlantic-Little, Brown, Boston, 1955, p. 119.

CHAPTER SIX
1. Blackstone, op. cit. vol. IV, p. 151.
2. Zechariah Chafee, Jr., *Free Speech and Free Press*, Harvard University Press, Cambridge, 1941, p. 10.
3. Cooley, op. cit. pp. 603–4.
4. The Constitution of Sweden, Chapter 4, Article 3.
5. Nieman Reports, April 1955, p. 10.
6. Near *v.* Minnesota, 283 U.S. Reports, 697 (1931).
7. Chafee, *Free Speech and Free Press*, op. cit. p. 381.
8. *The Federalist*, vol. II, p. 157.

CHAPTER SEVEN
1. James Morton Smith, 'The Sedition Law, Free Speech and the American Political Process,' *William & Mary Quarterly*, October 1952, p. 497.
2. Macaulay, op. cit. vol. I, p. 269.
3. Michael St. John Packe, *Life of John Stuart Mill*, The Macmillan Company, New York, 1955, p. 13.
4. James Morton Smith, 'The *Aurora* and the Sedition Laws,' *The Pennsylvania Magazine of History & Biography*, January 1953, p. 3.
5. James Morton Smith, 'History of the Alien and Sedition Laws,' unpublished ms., p. 239.
6. Zechariah Chafee, Jr., *Free Speech in the United States*, Harvard University Press, 1946, p. 513.
7. John Bach McMaster, *A History of the People of the United States*, D. Appleton and Company, New York, 1914, vol. II, p. 462.
8. James Morton Smith, 'History of the Alien and Sedition Laws,' ms. p. 135.
9. Ibid. ms. p. 375.
10. Elmer Davis, *History of the New York Times*, 1921, p. 347.
11. Ibid. p. 350.

12. James Morton Smith, 'The *Aurora* and the Sedition Law,' op. cit. p. 9.

13. James Morton Smith, 'The Case of John Daly Burk and His New York "Time Piece," ' *The Journalism Quarterly*, Winter 1953, p. 23.

14. The Editors of *La Prensa, Defense of Freedom*, John Day, New York, 1952, p. 129.

15. Chafee, *Free Speech in the United States*, op. cit. p. 10.

CHAPTER EIGHT

1. Arthur Aspinwall, *Politics and the Press 1780–1850*, Horne & Van Tal, London, 1948, p. 383.

2. Editors of *La Prensa*, op. cit. p. 84.

3. Ibid. pp. 83–91.

4. Ibid. p. 110.

5. *Paper for Printing*, UNESCO, Paris, 1952, p. 80.

6. Ibid. p. 88.

7. Raymond B. Nixon, 'Trends in Daily Newspaper Ownership Since 1945,' *Journalism Quarterly*, Winter 1954, p. 3.

8. Svend Thorsen, *Newspapers in Denmark*, Cophenhagen, 1953, p. 34.

9. Alexis de Tocqueville, *Democracy In America*, Alfred A. Knopf, New York, 1945, vol. 1, p. 186.

CHAPTER NINE

1. Justice Holmes, Dissenting Opinion in U.S. Ex rel, Milwaukee Pub. Co. *v.* Burleson, 255 U.S. 437 (1922).

2. Margaret L. Coit, *John C. Calhoun*, Houghton Mifflin Co., Boston, 1950, p. 308.

3. McMaster, op. cit. vol. VI, p. 288.

4. Chafee, *Government and Mass Communications*, op. cit. p. 292.

5. 327 U.S. Reports at 157–58.

6. 149 F 2d 511 (D.C. Cir 1945).

7. *News Letter On Intellectual Freedom*, Intellectual Freedom Committee of the American Library Association, June 1955, vol. III, no. 4.

8. Edward De Grazia, 'Obscenity and The Mail: A Study in Administrative Restraint,' *Law and Contemporary Problems*, Duke University School of Law, vol. XX, no. 4, p. 619.

CHAPTER TEN

1. *The Writings of Thomas Jefferson*, Andrew Liscomb (ed.), Thomas Jefferson Memorial Association, Washington, 1904, vol. XI, p. 225.
2. Alexis de Tocqueville, *Democracy in America*, Alfred A. Knopf, New York, 1945, vol. I, p. 185.
3. William Allen White, *Autobiography*, The Macmillan Company, New York, 1946, p. 126.
4. Oswald Garrison Villard, *The Disappearing Daily*, Alfred A. Knopf, New York, 1944, p. 5.
5. Malcolm W. Klein and Nathan Maccoby, *The Journalism Quarterly*, Summer 1954, p. 285.
6. Robert Batlin, *Journalism Quarterly*, Winter 1954, p. 297.
7. Charles Higbie, *Journalism Quarterly*, Winter 1954, p. 56.
8. Henry Luther Stoddard, *Horace Greeley*, G. P. Putnam & Sons, New York, 1946, p. 64.
9. Walter Gieber, 'Do Newspapers Overplay Negative News,' *Journalism Quarterly*, Summer 1955, p. 311.
10. Rebecca West, *The Meaning of Treason*, Viking Press, New York, 1947, p. 56.
11. Raymond B. Nixon, 'Changes in Reader Attitudes Toward Daily Newspapers,' *Journalism Quarterly*, Fall 1954, p. 421.
12. Herbert Luethy, *France Against Herself*, Frederick A. Praeger, New York, 1955, p. 91.

# INDEX

235